SAUDI ARABIA

MODERN
NATIONS
—OF THE—
WORLD

SAUDI ARABIA

BY WILLIAM GOODWIN

LUCENT BOOKS
P.O. BOX 289011
SAN DIEGO, CA 92198-9011

Dedicated to King Fahd, the most coherent voice for peace in the Middle East.

Library of Congress Cataloging-in-Publication Data

Goodwin, William, 1943–
    Saudi Arabia / by William Goodwin.
      p. cm. — (Modern nations of the world)
Includes bibliographical references (p.) and index.
    ISBN 1-56006-763-2 (hardcover)
    1. Saudi Arabia—Juvenile literature. [1. Saudi Arabia.] I. Title. II. Series.
    DS204.25 .G66 2001
    953.8—dc21

                                         00-010555

Copyright © 2001 by Lucent Books, Inc.
P.O. Box 289011, San Diego, CA 92198-9011
Printed in the U.S.A.

CONTENTS

INTRODUCTION

A LAND OF CHANGE AND TRADITION

When the desert kingdom of Saudi Arabia sprang into existence in 1932, Ibn Saud, its founder and first king, ruled a land with few known resources and a people who were mostly poor and uneducated. The country had few cities and virtually no industry. Although the sacred shrines of Islam generated income from the religious pilgrims who visited them every year, this revenue was not enough to lift the people of Saudi Arabia out of poverty.

All this changed in the late 1930s when geologists from the United States discovered oil under the flat gravel plains in the eastern part of the country. Saudi Arabia's oil deposits proved to be the largest on earth; in a single generation, the wealth that flowed from the wells transformed the poor kingdom into a prosperous and influential nation. Money from oil brought with it enormous changes, and Saudi Arabia became an experiment in how to rapidly develop a poor country. Within a few decades Saudi Arabia went from a mostly nomadic tribal society to a powerful kingdom run by financiers and billionaires capable of influencing economies around the world.

The flood of money brought by the discovery of oil changed ancient patterns of living in Saudi Arabia. With wealth came European and other influences that challenged and forever altered the Saudi Arabians' way of life, political system, and individual values. Almost overnight, a mostly nomadic people became a mostly urban people. Today the standard of living is much higher than it was half a century ago, and nutrition, welfare, material possessions, and education are all vastly improved. But the kingdom has had its share of growing pains. The immense cultural changes still sweeping the country have created deep divisions among Saudi Arabians, and the growing number of foreigners who have come to work and live in Saudi Arabia are a source of resentment for many citizens.

Through all the great upheavals of the last half-century, one aspect of Saudi Arabian life has not changed: its devotion to Islam. Saudi Arabia is the spiritual center of the Islamic world. It is custodian of Islam's most sacred shrines at Mecca and Medina and a guiding force for other Islamic nations. Saudi Arabians adhere to the strictist form of Islam, and their unwavering faith has shaped the country's response to its vast new wealth.

Saudi Arabia's prominence in world affairs has not altered the way most Saudis view themselves. The people of modern

The desert kingdom of Saudi Arabia struggled financially until the late 1930s, when geologists discovered oil there.

Muslim pilgrims read from the Quran during a visit to the holy city of Mecca.

Saudi Arabia possess a proud and noble heritage. Their ancestors arose from the early Semite civilization and were strongly influenced by the Greek, Roman, Egyptian, and Persian cultures. Noted historian Philip Hitti writes, "As the probable cradle of the Semitic family, the Arabian peninsula nursed those peoples who later migrated into the Fertile Crescent and subsequently became the Babylonians, the Assyrians, the Phoenicians, and the Hebrews of history."[1] Islam and tribal relationships dating back many centuries continue to be the guiding force in Saudi Arabia today.

GEOGRAPHY, NATURAL RESOURCES, CLIMATE, FLORA AND FAUNA

1

Other than around widely scattered oases, the vast interior of Saudi Arabia is too arid to support permanent settlements. But it would be incorrect to assume that this ancient land consists solely of inhospitable deserts. Within modern Saudi Arabia are bustling cities, cool mountain resorts, clustered tents of nomads, villages surrounded by date groves, seaports sheltered by coral reefs, and gravel plains overlying the world's richest oil deposits. A land of contrasts, this modern kingdom is difficult to know well, and it requires patience to discover the beauty and secrets of Saudi Arabia.

Saudi Arabia is located in southwestern Asia at the southern edge of the region often referred to as the Middle East. The kingdom of Saudi Arabia shares boundaries with seven countries and has coastlines on two bodies of water. Notably, Saudi Arabia is one of the few countries in the modern world that still has significant sections of its borders undefined. In the west, Saudi Arabia's boundary is defined by the waters of the Red Sea, which forms a coastline about 1,110 miles long. The Red Sea coast runs approximately north and south, and includes a number of small islands. To the north, Saudi Arabia is bounded by the countries of Jordan, Iraq, and Kuwait. The northern boundary extends almost 860 miles from the Gulf of Aqaba in the west to Ras al Khafji, just below Kuwait on the Persian Gulf. Saudi Arabia's eastern boundary follows the Persian Gulf from Ras al Khafji south to the peninsula of Qatar. Along the southeastern coast of the Arabian Peninsula, Saudi Arabia shares a border with the state of Oman that runs east and west through the Empty Quarter (Rub al Khali). Part of this southeastern border near Al Buraymi Oasis where the frontiers of Oman, Abu Dhabi

9

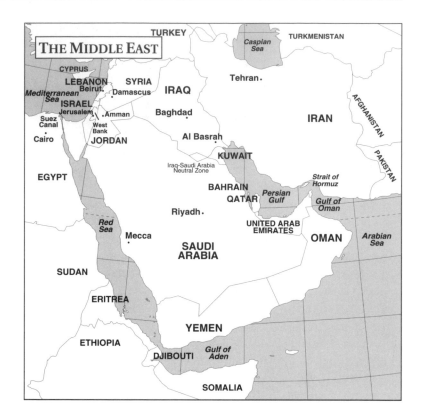

(one of the states of the United Arab Emirates), and Saudi
Arabia meet, is still not defined and remains a subject of dis-
pute between the three countries. The southern border of
Saudi Arabia west of the Empty Quarter is shared with the
country of Yemen.

TOPOGRAPHY AND NATURAL REGIONS

The underlying rock of the Arabian Peninsula is a very old
geological structure that developed at the same time that the
peaks of the Alps were being thrust upward in Europe. Geologic movements tilted the entire mass of the Arabian Peninsula so that today it slants downward from west to east, with
the highest places in the west adjacent to an immense fault
in the earth's crust. This fault, called the Great Rift, formed
the Red Sea, a deep sliver of ocean that is connected to the
Mediterranean Sea by the Suez Canal. Geologists believe that
the Arabian Peninsula is slowly rotating counterclockwise in
a way that will, in approximately 10 million years, close off
the Persian Gulf and make it a salt lake.

On the Arabian Peninsula, the eastern line of the Great Rift has created a steep and, in places, high line of mountains and hills that run parallel to the Red Sea between the Gulf of Aqaba in the north and the Gulf of Aden in the south. While the western side of this line of mountains is steep, the slope eastward is relatively gentle, dropping gradually to the exposed bedrock of the ancient landmass that existed before the faulting occurred. In the middle of the country a lower set of hills, the Jabal Tuwayq, runs north and south through the area of Riyadh, the capital city.

Saudi Arabia has been historically divided into a number of geographical zones that to this day define unique areas of the kingdom. The northern half of the peninsula adjacent to the Red Sea is known as the Hijaz. Below the Hijaz on the more rugged southern half of the peninsula is a region called Asir. In Asir a coastal plain, called the Tihamah, rises from the coast of the Red Sea to the base of the nearby mountains. Asir extends southward to the borders of the rugged terrain of Yemen. In the center of Saudi Arabia is a plateau called Najd, which extends east to and slightly beyond the Jabal Tuwayq. North of Najd a larger desert, An Nafud, isolates the heart of the Arabian Peninsula from the steppes of northern Arabia. South of Najd lies one of the largest sand deserts in the world, the Rub al Khali (the Empty Quarter). A long, narrow strip of inhospitable desert known as Ad Dahna separates Najd from eastern Arabia. The easternmost part of the country consists of gravel and sand coastal plains where vast oil deposits have been found in the underlying rocks.

THE HIJAZ AND ASIR

The western coastal high ground consists of northern and southern mountain ranges separated by a less mountainous area near the Islamic holy city of Mecca. The northern range of the Hijaz mountains occasionally exceeds seven thousand feet in height, but the elevation gradually decreases toward the south to about two thousand feet around Mecca. The steep western side of these mountains drops abruptly to the Red Sea, often with only a narrow coastal plain separating the mountains from the water. There are no natural harbors along Saudi Arabia's Red Sea coastline, although there are important man-made harbors at Al Yanbu and Jeddah.

The eastern slopes of the mountains near Medina are marked by wadis, dry riverbeds that follow the courses of ancient rivers.

The western slopes of the mountains have been stripped of soil by erosion from infrequent but torrential rainfall. The less steep eastern slopes are marked by dry riverbeds, called wadis, that follow the courses of ancient rivers. These wadis still lead runoff from the rare rainfalls down to the plains. A number of scattered settlements, Medina being by far the largest and most important, are able to draw sufficient water from springs and wells in the vicinity of these wadis to support significant amounts of agriculture on the eastern slopes.

South of Mecca, the mountains rise sharply again, often exceeding eight thousand feet above sea level, and several peaks approach ten thousand feet. The rugged western face of the southern mountains drops quickly to a coastal plain, called the Tihamah lowlands, that averages forty miles in width. Along this southern seacoast, a salty tidal plain provides limited agricultural opportunities, but just a short distance inland rich alluvial plains allow productive farming. The relatively well-watered and fertile upper slopes of these plains and the mountains behind them have been extensively terraced to allow maximum land use.

The gentle eastern slope of the mountain range in Asir gradually becomes a plateau that slopes southward toward the Empty Quarter. Although rainfall is infrequent in this area, a number of fertile wadis, the most important being the Wadi Bishah and the Wadi Tathlith, make agriculture possible on a relatively large scale. A number of solidified lava flows carve lifeless swaths across the surfaces of the plateaus east of the mountain ranges in the Hijaz and Asir, evidence of fairly recent volcanic activity in Saudi Arabia.

NAJD

In the center of the peninsula east of Hijaz and Asir lies Najd, a rocky plateau with sections of small, sandy deserts and isolated groups of mountains. The best known of the mountainous areas is the Jabal Shammar, located northwest of Riyadh and just south of the An Nafud. This region is home to the pastoral Shammar tribes. Today their former capital, the large oasis of Hail, is a flourishing urban center of Najd.

The Najd plateau slopes downward from an elevation of four thousand five hundred feet in the west to two thousand five hundred feet at its easternmost limit. A number of wadis cross the region from west to east, and, as in other areas of Saudi Arabia, provide enough subsurface water to supply agricultural needs.

Sixty million years ago, a thick layer of limestone formed at the bottom of a shallow sea where the vast deserts of central Saudi Arabia are now. Today, not far from Riyadh, those limestone formations are riddled with countless caves and holes known in Arabic as dahls. Since their discovery by amateur cave explorers in the 1980s, many beautiful and unusual dahls have been found in this area, and the Saudi government has undertaken a program to protect the caves from harm.

In the heart of Najd is the region known as the Jabal Tuwayq, an arc-shaped ridge of mountains with a steep west face that rises more than eight hundred feet above the plateau. Many oasis towns exist in this area, the most important of which are Buraydah, Unayzah, Riyadh, and Al Kharj. Outside the oasis areas, however, Najd is sparsely populated. Large salt marshes are also found throughout the region.

NORTHERN ARABIA

An area of steppes, geographically a part of the Syrian Desert, is found north of the An Nafud desert. This region, known as Badiyat ash Sham, consists of an upland plateau cut by numerous wadis, most running northeastward toward Iraq. Covered with seasonal grass and scrub vegetation, this area is used by nomadic and seminomadic herders as pastureland for their camels, goats, and sheep. The most significant feature of the Badiyat ash Sham is a large basin named Wadi as Sirhan, once an ancient inland sea, that dips to almost one thousand feet below the surrounding plateau. For thousands of years, some of the heavily traveled caravan routes between the Mediterranean and the Arabian Peninsula passed through the Wadi as Sirhan.

EASTERN ARABIA

Eastern Arabia (east of the Ad Dahna desert) is sometimes called Al Hasa after the great oasis of the same name, one of the most fertile oases of the country. East of the desert lies the rocky As Summan plateau, about seventy-five miles wide. Except for the occasional oasis (Al Hasa and Al Hufuf being the most important), this area is a barren terrain of

highly eroded surfaces, ancient river gorges, and isolated buttes.

Farther east the terrain changes abruptly to the flat lowlands of the coastal plain running north and south along the Persian Gulf. This area, averaging thirty-seven miles wide, is generally featureless and covered with gravel and sand. In the north is the Ad Dibdibah gravel plain and in the south the Al Jafurah sand desert, which reaches the Gulf near Dhahran and merges with the Empty Quarter at its southern end.

The flatlands of the coastal plain edge down to the sea forming an extremely irregular coastline where sandy plains and salt flats merge almost imperceptibly with the waters of the Persian Gulf. Because most of the area is barely above sea level, the land surface is unstable. The Persian Gulf is shallow here, with shoals and reefs extending far offshore. At Ras Tanura, where more oil is pumped into oil tankers than anywhere else in the world, very long piers and jetties that extend into deep water are required to dock the supertankers that carry the oil to world markets.

THE GREAT DESERTS

Three great deserts isolate Najd from the lands to the north, east, and south. In the north, the great An Nafud desert covers 21,450 square miles with an average elevation of three thousand three hundred feet. Long sand dunes, twenty to forty miles in length with ridges as much as three hundred feet high separated by valleys as wide as ten miles, characterize the An Nafud. Iron oxide gives the sand a red tint. This area has several oases, and seasonal rains bring up short-lived but succulent grasses that permit nomadic herding during the winter and spring.

Stretching in a narrow arc more than eighty miles south from the An Nafud is the Ad Dahna, a narrow band of sand mountains described by early explorers as a "river of sand." Like the An Nafud, its sand tends to be reddish, particularly in the north where it is blown into long, narrow dunes. Although water is scarcer here than in the An Nafud, the Ad Dahna has just enough to supply the nomadic Bedouin with winter and spring pasture for their sheep and camels.

The southern portion of the Ad Dahna curves westward along the ridge of the Jabal Tuwayq. At its southern end, it merges with the Empty Quarter, one of the truly forbidding

THE EMPTY QUARTER: ONE OF THE LAST UNEXPLORED PLACES ON EARTH

The entire southern portion of Saudi Arabia, an area larger than France, consists of the largest uninterrupted sand desert in the world. The Empty Quarter, called the Rub al Khali in Arabic, covers more than 215,000 square miles, and shows surprising variety. In the west, where the desert surface is elevated about 2,000 feet above sea level, the sand is fine and soft; in the east, the elevation drops to about 600 feet and much of the surface is covered by relatively stable sheets of sand and extensive salt flats. In places, particularly in the east, long sand dunes prevail; elsewhere, sand mountains as high as 950 feet form complex patterns.

With droughts that frequently last more than ten years, virtually no plant or animal life survives here. The few nomadic Bedouin who inhabit the area during cooler seasons simply call the Empty Quarter "Ar Ra-malah," which means "the Sand." In the eastern sector of the Empty Quarter, mountains of sand more than 800 feet high and 30 miles in length have been observed.

Until the 1950s, when oil companies began exploring this desolate region, the Empty Quarter was almost entirely uncharted. Since then, numerous expeditions have mapped the area, and in 1975 Al Ghawar, one of the largest oil deposits in the world, was found there.

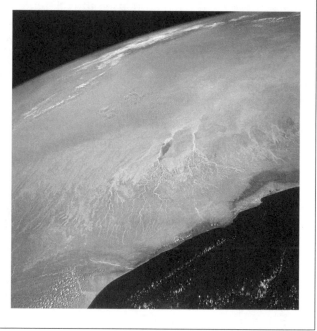

The Empty Quarter, seen here in a satellite image, was almost completely uncharted until the 1950s.

sand deserts of the world and, until the 1950s, one of the least explored. Most of the area is totally waterless and un-inhabited except for a few wandering Bedouin tribes.

NATURAL RESOURCES

Beneath Saudi Arabia's eastern deserts and the seafloor off the eastern coast exist the largest proven reserves of oil on earth. These huge deposits make the country the world's largest oil producer. The United States alone receives from

Saudi Arabia between 1 and 2 million barrels of crude oil every day, more than 15 percent of the oil imported by the United States each year. Given its high production levels (equal to about 13 percent of the world's total oil production) and the kingdom's small domestic need for oil, Saudi Arabia's domination of international crude oil markets is unchallenged. With over 260 billion barrels of proven oil reserves (one-fourth of the world's total) and possibly as much as 1 trillion barrels of ultimately recoverable oil, Saudi Arabia is likely to retain its present position as the world's largest oil producer for many years to come.

Natural gas is usually found with oil, and so it is not surprising that Saudi Arabia ranks fifth in the world in natural gas deposits. The government is increasing gas production to supply

A pipeline in Saudi Arabia, a country that is responsible for about 13 percent of the world's total oil production, transports oil to a tanker.

the country's growing petrochemical industry as well as to generate electricity, desalinate seawater, and power other industrial facilities, including those previously powered by oil.

Although the presence of so much oil and gas overshadows the development of other mineral resources, Saudi Arabia also has some deposits of other minerals. Small but active gold and silver mines and significant quantities of iron, gypsum, phosphorite, salt, and other minerals are found in Saudi Arabia.

WATER RESOURCES

With no permanent rivers or lakes and only a very small amount of surface water, Saudi Arabia must meet its water needs with rainfall, groundwater, and desalinated seawater. In eastern Arabia and in the Jabal Tuwayq region of central Arabia, artesian wells and springs are plentiful. In the eastern province of Al Hasa many large, deep oases are constantly filled by artesian springs. Such oases and wells permit extensive irrigation in many eastern areas of the country. In the Hijaz and Asir regions in the west, wells are abundant, and springs are common in the mountainous areas. In Najd and the great deserts, water sources are relatively rare and widely scattered. Water there must be hoisted or pumped to the surface, and its quality is often poor.

Because of the shortage of surface water in Saudi Arabia, new sources of water were essential for development. Technicians from the Saudi Arabian Oil Company (Aramco) found abundant water in very deep layers of porous rock called aquifers in northern and eastern Arabia. One such aquifer, the Wasia, is the largest aquifer in Saudi Arabia, containing more water than the entire Persian Gulf. During the last quarter of the twentieth century, all of Saudi Arabia's large-scale agricultural projects relied primarily on these deep aquifers.

Most of the total water demand in Saudi Arabia is consumed by agriculture. The deep aquifers supplying this water contain what is called "fossil water," water accumulated during an earlier geologic age. Fossil water is nonrenewable; someday, like Saudi Arabia's oil, it will run out. For this reason the Saudi government has invested heavily in desalinating seawater. In 2000, most of the country's drinking water was produced by desalination, as Saudi Arabia's twenty-two plants produced 30 percent of all the desalinated water in the world.

THE OASIS: MAKING LIFE POSSIBLE IN THE DESERT

An oasis is a fertile region in an otherwise arid desert where the all-year presence of a water source makes agriculture possible. In the west of Saudi Arabia, the most important oasis town is Medina, and in the east Al Hasa and Al Hufuf are the most important centers that began as desert oases. Some oases in Saudi Arabia have enough water to support a major town and organized commercial agriculture; others support little more than a few families, their sheep and camels, and perhaps a date grove. Date palms, in fact, constitute the primary plant life of an oasis both as shade for other crops that cannot survive in the direct Arabian sun and as a great source of food in themselves.

Underground sources provide the water for Saudi Arabian oases. In some places the oasis water source is merely a small spring, but in other cases, like Al Hufuf, artesian wells fill large pools with warm, clear water that is diverted into extensive irrigation channels to irrigate date palms, citrus, fig, peach, and apricot trees, vegetables, and cereal crops such as wheat, barley, and millet.

CLIMATE

With the exception of the province of Asir on the west coast, Saudi Arabia has a desert climate characterized by extreme heat during the day, an abrupt drop in temperature at night, and small amounts of unpredictable rainfall. Because of variable subtropical high-pressure systems, wide range of altitudes, and the influences of the Red Sea and Persian Gulf, temperature and humidity vary greatly from region to region and from season to season. The greatest temperature extremes are found between the coastal lowlands, the high mountains, and the arid plateaus.

Along the coastal regions of the Red Sea and the Persian Gulf, the desert climate is a bit cooler and more humid due to the effects of these large bodies of water. On these coasts, temperatures seldom rise above 100°F, but the relative humidity usually exceeds 85 percent and frequently reaches 100 percent. This condition produces a hot mist during the day and a warm fog at night. Prevailing winds are from the north, and as long as the breezes blow, the coastal areas are tolerable in the summer and pleasant in the winter. Winds coming from any direction other than north generally spell trouble. These seasonal winds tend to be strong and can affect large parts of the country. The various winds are so distinctive that epic stories and famous poems have been written about them. The south wind brings an increase in temperature and humidity, and when it blows especially hard, it gives rise to a kind of storm known around the Gulf as a kauf. In late spring and early summer a strong northwesterly wind, called a shamal, blows. Shamals, which are particularly severe in eastern Saudi Arabia, produce choking sand and dust storms that can decrease visibility to zero. A particularly unpleasant version of the shamal occurs when a foglike dust storm combines with a light rain to make an airborne mud storm.

A uniform climate prevails in Najd and other central regions of the country, including the great deserts. The average summer temperature is 113°F in central Saudi Arabia, but high temperatures of 130°F are not uncommon. During the summer the heat becomes intense as soon as the sun rises and lasts until sunset. Nights are, by comparison, cool. Winter in central Saudi Arabia seldom brings freezing temperatures, but the lack of humidity combined with a high windchill factor makes

Most of Saudi Arabia has a desert climate characterized by extreme heat during the day and an abrupt drop in temperature at night.

some nights bitterly cold here. In the spring and autumn, high temperatures average around 84°F in central Saudi Arabia.

The region of Asir in the southwest usually receives considerable rainfall from the Indian Ocean monsoon between October and March. An average of twelve inches of rain falls over most of Asir during this period, which accounts for more than half of the region's total annual rainfall. Additionally, in Asir and the southern Hijaz, considerable condensation caused by the cool temperatures in the higher mountains contributes to the total available water.

For the rest of the country, rainfall is low and undependable. An entire year's rainfall may come in the form of one or two torrential outbursts that flood the wadis and then rapidly disappear into the soil where the water is trapped above layers of impervious rock. This usually provides enough groundwater to sustain the growth of grass and brush for the many nomadic people who move their herds from region to region in an endless quest for forage and water. Although the average rainfall is four inches a year in most of Saudi Arabia, whole regions may not receive measurable rain for several years in a row. When such droughts occur, as they did in the north in 1957 and 1958, the affected areas become quite incapable of sustaining life, either animals or agriculture.

FLORA AND FAUNA

The plants and animals of Saudi Arabia exhibit remarkable adaptations to the arid desert conditions. Animals, often hidden underground by day, tend to be invisible to the casual observer. Plants and trees are generally confined to the irrigated areas around oases.

The date palm grows almost everywhere in Saudi Arabia where there is water. This tree is such an integral and traditional part of the Saudi Arabian experience that it is prominently featured on the nation's coat of arms. Besides date palms, mimosas, and acacias, the Arabian Peninsula is almost devoid of trees. Trees are so rare, in fact, that the standard Arabic word for tree, *shajar*, is used by nomadic Bedouin to describe a type of small bush that sheep and camels graze upon. Grasses can be found in many areas following rains, and numerous flowering plants are native to the mountainous areas of Saudi Arabia. Cactus and aloe

A herder leads his donkey and a flock of sheep through the arid Saudi Arabian desert.

grow abundantly in some areas. Arabia was the world's primary source of incense in ancient times and it still produces a number of aromatic herbs and gums.

Most of the plants of the Arabian Peninsula grow in oases, whose inhabitants would have been isolated from other oases and seasonal pastures had it not been for the camel. The camel is the traditional mainstay of nomadic life; for millennia the tribal people of the Arabian Peninsula depended on the camel for milk, food, clothing, fuel (from its dried dung), transportation, and power for drawing water from deep wells and for plowing. Today the camel is less important, but still valued as livestock.

Domestic animals, including camels, sheep, and goats, are the most visible animals in Saudi Arabia, most numerous in rural areas . Mutton and lamb are the favorite meat of most Saudis, and goat milk makes their best cheese.

Gazelles, oryx, and ibex once ranged the plains of Saudi Arabia, much as they still do in Africa. Uncontrolled hunting, however, has made these animals extinct in Arabia; today they are found only in zoos and special farms. Hyenas, wolves, and jackals can still be found in some areas, but the African lion, once common on the peninsula, is now extinct in Saudi Arabia. Baboons, foxes, rabbits, hedgehogs, gerbils, and other small mammals can still be found in some parts of the country. Ostriches are extinct in Saudi Arabia but eagles, vultures, and owls are quite common. Flamingos, pelicans, egrets, and other waterfowl frequent the coastal areas. Many smaller birds inhabit the towns and oases. Deadly desert snakes, including horned vipers and cobras, are common in some areas. Poisonous sea snakes are abundant in both the Persian Gulf and the Red Sea.

THE AMAZING DHUBB

Forget the "ship of the desert" (a name often applied to the camel). The dhubb may just be the animal best adapted to life in the deserts of Arabia.

The dhubb can go a lifetime without drinking water; it gets all it needs from the fluids in the bugs and small plants it eats. Another of this large, iguanalike lizard's adaptations to desert life allows it to eat less because it needs no energy to maintain a constant body temperature; it is perfectly comfortable in whatever the surrounding temperature is. In the early morning when the air is cool, the dhubb's skin is baggy and dark gray, the better to absorb the warmth of the sun. When it is hot and bright, the dhubb's skin becomes smooth and tight and light colored to cut down on solar energy absorption. These lizards are most active when the temperature is over 100°F!

When some creature, probably suffering from heat stroke, tries to bother a dhubb, the big reptile inflates its already large self to a truly fearsome size and hisses ferociously. In view of its intimidating size, scary call, tail spikes, and powerful jaws, few animals or people want to mess with a dhubb. And just in case things get a little too rough, the dhubb can always retreat into its hole, which it digs deep into the desert floor.

Hunting has driven oryxes, ostriches, and gazelles to extinction on the Arabian Peninsula, and many fear the perfectly adapted dhubbs are next.

THE CORAL REEFS OF THE RED SEA

The warm, crystal clear waters of the Red Sea support an immense variety of sea life, including extensive coral reefs. Coral growth is hampered by freshwater runoff and by large waves, and the coast of Saudi Arabia has very little of either. As a result the coral here grows into spectacular and delicate formations. The sea life that lives around these coral reefs is abundant and diverse, and many species are found only in the Red Sea.

The Red Sea separates the Arabian Peninsula and Africa, and runs approximately north and south for about one thousand three hundred miles from Suez, Egypt, to the Gulf of Aden, where it connects with the Indian Ocean. While coral grows everywhere in the Red Sea, reef formation is most extensive in the warmer southern half, where coral grows so fast that it intrudes on ship channels, which must be blasted and dredged from time to time to keep up with the coral growth.

Because of the abundance of life forms and the clarity of the water, snorkeling and scuba diving are popular, especially around the Red Sea port city of Jeddah. Underwater explorers, including the Austrian Hans Hass in the 1950s and later the French coinventor of scuba, Jacques Cousteau, have declared the Red Sea to be among the most beautiful and exciting places in the world to dive.

Why is this sea of clear turquoise water called the Red Sea? More poetic observers would say the name comes from the scarlet reflection of the setting sun as it dips below the horizon on the African side of the Red Sea. Some marine biologists, on the other hand, have attributed the red in the sea's name to a type of floating algae, which sometimes leaves a dull red scum on the surface of the water.

The danger of pollution is always present in the almost landlocked Red Sea, particularly from oil spillage. A decree from the king of Saudi Arabia forbids the discharge of any pollutants, including oil, within one hundred miles of the Saudi Arabian coastline. Nevertheless, oily sludge washes ashore on the beaches from time to time.

A CULTURE SHAPED BY GEOGRAPHY

The desert is the most prominent geographical feature of the Arabian Peninsula. Though vast expanses of arid land dominate Saudi Arabia, the country also has long stretches of coastline along the Persian Gulf and the Red Sea and numerous oases that are productive agricultural centers. The differences in living conditions between the coast and the desert set the stage for the national character of Saudi Arabia to develop in two different directions.

The Rise of Urban Centers and Islam

The modern nation of Saudi Arabia occupies most of the Arabian Peninsula, a land where nomadic tribes have lived for at least four thousand years. The harsh desert environment helped shape the culture that would become Saudi Arabia, but the early Arabians were also strongly influenced by the early civilizations of Europe, Africa, and Asia. From the earliest times the ancestors of today's Saudi Arabians had close contact with the people and ideas of Mesopotamia (the Tigris-Euphrates River Valley), Egypt, Persia, Greece, and the Roman Empire. From these lands came seagoing traders, caravans of merchants, and pilgrims who visited the Arabian shores of the Red Sea and the Persian Gulf and traveled through the interior of Arabia on ancient trade routes. These visitors all contributed to the formation of the distinctive culture that would become Saudi Arabia.

The Pre-Islamic Period

Archaeological evidence indicates that the earliest inhabitants of Arabia were nomads from regions to the north that now are parts of Jordan and Iraq. The earliest permanent settlements appeared along the coasts of the Red Sea and Persian Gulf, possibly due to the terrible droughts that still plague the interior of the peninsula.

The bodies of water on either side of the Arabian Peninsula, the Red Sea and the Persian Gulf, provided seagoing access to the nearby river-valley civilizations of the Nile (in present-day Egypt) and the Tigris-Euphrates (in modern Iraq). Evidence dating back to 3000 B.C. shows that extensive trade in agricultural products, spices, textiles, gold, and frankincense existed between the early inhabitants of the Arabian Peninsula and the rich civilizations of the Nile and Tigris-Euphrates.

Living conditions of the people of Arabia's interior regions began to improve around 1000 B.C. when the camel saddle was invented. This allowed camels to be used to transport large loads, and since the camel was the only animal that could cross the great expanses of empty, arid land, the desert dwellers were now able to benefit from the trade that had previously skirted Arabia.

The growth in trade between the Nile and Tigris-Euphrates civilizations passing through the Arabian Peninsula brought prosperity to parts of the region. The climate and topography of the southwestern coastal areas permitted greater agricultural development than was possible in other parts of the peninsula, and so Arabia's first urban centers, based on trade and agriculture, developed there.

The early city inhabitants of Arabia's southwestern coast lived in small kingdoms or city-states. Saba (often called Sheba, mentioned frequently in the Bible) was the best known of these kingdoms because of its wealth from spices and agriculture. Noting the prosperity of the southwestern corner of the Arabian Peninsula, the Romans called the area Arabia Felix (literally, "Happy Arabia").

As trade across Arabian lands increased, urban centers appeared in the interior of the peninsula, too. Most of these towns began as stops for the great camel caravans on their long trips across the desert, and some of these settlements became religious and cultural centers as well. The most successful of these was Mecca, where several nearby shrines to the deities of the region's polytheistic religions became destinations for pilgrimages by Arabs from all over the peninsula.

A variety of religious traditions have existed in Arabia since the dawn of history. Prior to the birth of Islam in the seventh century A.D., polytheistic and pagan practices were widespread, especially in the western part of the peninsula. In addition to the local pagan practices, traders from other lands brought many other religious influences to Arabia. The city of Najran in southwestern Arabia, for example, came to be ruled in A.D. 500 by a Jewish king, yet the town had a Christian church with a bishop, monks, priests, nuns, and lay clergy. Jews played an important role in the development of both southwestern Arabia and the communities around the area of modern-day Medina.

CARAVANSERAI: OUTPOSTS IN THE DESERT

For many centuries, overland trade and religious pilgrimage routes crisscrossed Asia and North Africa. Most of these routes passed though vast deserts, where lack of water and the threat of bandits made travel precarious. To promote trade and protect pilgrims, local kingdoms would build fortified outposts, called caravanserais, where the camel caravans could rest, obtain water, and find safety.

Initially the caravanserai was a walled and gated fortlike structure with a well, stables, and sleeping accommodations, but as trade grew many caravanserais became local centers of commerce where the lively exchange of goods and ideas could take place. Some tribes began to build caravanserais on a grander scale with graceful arches and tall minarets for the mosques where devout Muslims could pray.

Today most of the thousands of caravanserais that once thrived in Arabia and other parts of Asia have fallen into ruin, but recently a renewed appreciation for their historical and architectural value has surfaced. Some have been restored and there are plans to turn others into museums or hotels.

THE EARLY ISLAMIC PERIOD

Modern Saudi Arabians, as well as many other Arabs and Muslims, trace much of their heritage to the teachings of the Islamic prophet Muhammad. Muhammad was born in A.D. 570 in Mecca at a time when this western Arabian city was a new and growing center of trade.

Despite new outside influences, the residents of Mecca still connected social standing with tribal connections. It is therefore highly significant that Muhammad was born into Mecca's leading tribe, the Quraysh. At the time of Muhammad's birth, the Quraysh enjoyed highly profitable trading alliances with tribes all over the peninsula. Because of their prominence as traders and their control of the region's water sources, the Quraysh were the dominant tribe in the region.

Following the death of his father when Muhammad was just a boy, Muhammad's uncle Abu Talib, sent the youth to the desert for five years. There he learned the traditional ways of Arabia from the desert-dwelling Bedouin tribes, ways prosperous Mecca had forgotten. Muhammad came to value Bedouin attributes like humility, hospitality, and toughness in the face of the difficult desert life. When he returned to Mecca he began working for Abu Talib in the caravan business, which provided an opportunity for him to travel beyond Arabia. Muhammad visited Christian and Jewish communities where he discovered the notion of Scripture and the belief in one God, ideas that would soon help him shape a new religion, Islam.

When he was twenty-five years old, after he had married a wealthy widow, Muhammad went alone into the mountains near Mecca where, according to Islamic belief, the angel Gabriel appeared to him. The angel commanded him to go to the people and recite verses from God that the angel was about to reveal to him. These verses would later make up part of the Islamic book of Scripture, the Quran, which means literally "the recitation." Muslims, as the people who accept the teachings of Muhammad call themselves, believe that Muhammad continued to receive revelations from God throughout his life, sometimes through the angel Gabriel and sometimes directly from God through dreams and visions.

From the beginning, Islam was as much a political as a religious force, and Muhammad became not only a prophet in the eyes of his followers but also a political and military leader. His calling began in the year 613 when he began publicly reciting the revelations he had received, according to Islamic belief, from God. The revelations attacked many religious customs prevalent in Arabia at the time, but the most controversial point of Muhammad's teachings was that there was only one God. This came into direct conflict with the worship of the numerous gods that made Mecca a profitable destination for many pilgrims.

At first the leaders of Mecca were not threatened by Muhammad's teachings, but by 618 he had gained enough followers that the Quraysh tribe probably would have killed him if he had not been under the protection of his powerful uncle, Abu Talib. The Quraysh did, in fact, attack those of Muhammad's followers who lacked powerful family connections, so Muhammad sent many of these vulnerable supporters to a kingdom in North Africa ruled by a sympathetic king. Then Abu Talib died in 619, and Muhammad was no longer safe in Mecca.

In 622 Muhammad, fearing he would be killed if he stayed in Mecca, fled the city of his birth. With his family and a band of followers, he traveled about two hundred miles north to the town of Yathrib. He resumed preaching in Yathrib, where he gained a great number of new believers. Eventually the date of Muhammad's flight from Mecca to Yathrib, called the hijira, came to mark the beginning of the Islamic calendar.

The Quraysh, not happy that Muhammad's belief in one God was finding so much acceptance in Yathrib, waged a number of battles against Muhammad's supporters. Muhammad proved to be a brilliant military leader capable of inspiring great courage in his soldiers. His armies grew rapidly and Muhammad eventually won the loyalty of most of the tribes in the region. Ultimately, the Quraysh were no match for the new army of Islam, and in 630 Muhammad returned triumphantly to Mecca. Muhammad's belief in one god became the religion of Mecca too, and soon all of western Arabia had adopted the new faith called Islam.

According to Muslim belief, Muhammad recited verses from God which were revealed to him by the angel Gabriel.

By his death in 632, Muhammad had united almost all of Arabia through various treaties, although not all of the tribes necessarily embraced Islamic beliefs. Those Christians and Jews who paid a special tax were allowed by Muhammad to keep their faith. Following his death, this practice continued, but those who still practiced polytheistic faiths were forced to become Muslims or be imprisoned. In this way Islam became the religion of most Arabs.

Because only he had received God's revelations, Muhammad had no spiritual successor, so after his death his leadership of the Islamic world was assumed by a series of kinglike caliphs. At first the caliphs governed the growing Islamic empire from Yathrib, which had been renamed Madinat an Nabi ("the city of the Prophet"), shortened to Medina.

The caliphs concentrated on extending the Islamic empire; to that end they waged almost continuous wars to spread the new faith. Arab tribes that had previously fought each other now united under Islamic beliefs, and the resulting army was

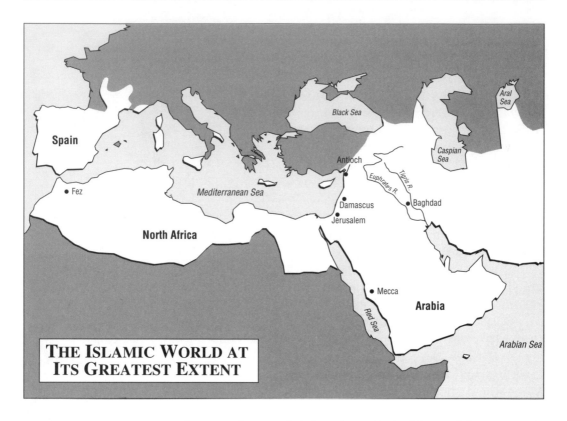

THE ISLAMIC WORLD AT ITS GREATEST EXTENT

so large and powerful that the caliphs felt confident enough to attack the Roman and Persian Empires. The Arab armies met with tremendous success, and they quickly conquered large areas of Asia, Europe, and North Africa. At its height, the Islamic empire extended from what is now Spain in the west to Pakistan in the east.

In 656 the third caliph, Uthman, was assassinated and his successor, Ali, turned his back on Medina and Mecca and moved his court to present-day Iraq. Following Ali, the caliphs ruled from Syria or Iraq, and control of the Islamic world was removed from Arabia.

THE ARABIAN MIDDLE AGES, 700–1500

For the next two hundred years, the centers of Islamic power remained in the Fertile Crescent, an arc of fertile land stretching from what is today Israel and Syria southeast to Iraq and the Persian Gulf. Then around 900 Islam's political center moved even farther away from Arabia when the successors to the caliphs established simultaneous capitals in Egypt, India, and what is now Turkey and the Central Asian republics. Mecca, however, remained the spiritual center of Islam, primarily because Mecca was the site of the pilgrimage that the Quran required all Muslims to make once in their lives.

As has happened in all of the world's major religions, differences of opinion and power struggles among early leaders of the faith led to a number of splits within Islam. The first split within the ranks of devout Muslims occurred as the result of an argument about who was the legitimate successor to the third caliph, Uthman. One segment of the population refused to accept the new caliph, Ali, as the legitimate heir of Muhammad. The supporters of Ali, who were called the Kharijites (from an Arabic word meaning "those who leave"), were unwilling to compromise and migrated to the eastern side of the Arabia peninsula. Although other Muslims frequently called the Kharijites bandits and assassins, Ali's supporters lived by strict notions of justice and piety. They believed that

Ali (center) and the caliphs, seen here battling against the Syrians, moved control of the Islamic world from Arabia to Syria and Iraq.

since Muhammad had been sent to bring righteousness to the world and to teach the Arabs to pray and distribute their wealth and power fairly, whoever failed to follow Muhammad's directives should be opposed or killed.

The ultraconservative Kharijite movement became the major religious influence along the Persian Gulf coast of Arabia from the ninth through eleventh centuries, and some aspects of Kharijite thinking have survived into the twenty-first century. The uncompromising strictness of the original Kharijites was typical of the intensity with which tribal Arabs had accepted and spread the beliefs of Islam. This fierce passion was the single most important factor in the success of the Arab armies in their conquests of the seventh century.

Ongoing power struggles between those who supported different leaders who all claimed to be the true descendants of Muhammad eventually led to several major Islamic sects, most importantly the Sunni and the Shia. Offshoots developed within these sects, too, including the Wahhabi branch of Sunni Islam, the most important form of Islam in modern Saudi Arabia.

The Wahhabi sect, born in the hostile desert environment where strict adherence to time-tested practices was crucial to survival, interprets Islam in a very strict sense. The Wahhabis eventually became the majority in Saudi Arabia, especially in the eastern regions of the Arabian Peninsula. Its members believe that many of the practices of non-Wahhabi Muslims reflect the old pagan rituals opposed by Muhammad. Given the Wahhabi belief in only one correct way of life, they naturally came into conflict with other Islamic sects, and from their earliest days the Wahhabis have been at odds with the country's Shia minority.

By the year 900, large numbers of Muslims were already making the pilgrimage to Mecca every year. They expected the caliph to protect Mecca, Medina, and other holy sites in the Hijaz as well as routes to them. As long as the caliph was strong, he could control the Hijaz, but as the caliph's control of Arabia began to slip, the western part of the peninsula became an easy target for raiders. In 930 the Shia minority, centered in the oasis town of Al Hufuf in eastern Arabia, was strong enough to successfully attack and plunder the major cities of Iraq to the north and fanatical enough to attack Mecca in the west. They removed the sacred stone of the

THE LINGERING INFLUENCE OF ARABIAN PAGAN BELIEFS

Before the appearance of Islam, the inhabitants of Arabia shared a constellation of beliefs that scholars such as Philip Hitti believe represent the most primitive forms of the Semitic family of faiths, a family of beliefs that eventually gave birth to the Jewish, Christian, and Islamic faiths.

Sun and moon worship, ornate temples, elaborate rituals, and animal sacrifices were common features of the pagan religions of pre-Islamic Arabian societies. Despite the efforts of Muhammad and his Muslim successors to eradicate pagan practices, many elements of the earlier religions seeped into Islam. The ancient black stone with its mysterious carvings that is set into the Ka'aba, the most important Islamic shrine in Mecca, is a prime example. As recently as a few centuries ago, various Islamic sects were still making offerings of garments and weapons to certain sacred trees in western Arabia and worshiping a variety of gods and goddesses at their shrines in the mountains near Mecca and Medina.

To this day, many Bedouin believe the desert is the home of demonlike creatures called jinns (sometimes spelled djinns). According to the ancient pagan beliefs, gods were generally friendly toward humans but the jinns, representing the terrors of the desert and its wild animal life, were hostile and dangerous. Islam has not succeeded in entirely eliminating the Bedouin's belief in these creatures, a belief that dates back to pagan days. Many still believe that jinns reign over the unknown parts of the world causing all sorts of disease and madness and frightening the daylights out of children.

Muslim pilgrims flock to the Ka'aba, the most important Islamic shrine in Mecca.

Ka'aba, the central shrine and primary destination of the Islamic pilgrimage, and stopped the pilgrimage for several years until the caliph agreed to pay a ransom to the Shia raiders for the return of the sacred stone.

In the Middle Ages, the desert region of Najd was isolated from the outer world, while along the coast the Hijaz experienced waves of outside influence from traders traveling both by sea and land. Najd, more arid and barren than western Arabia, was surrounded on three sides by deserts and separated from the Hijaz by rugged mountains. For a while several important overland routes to the Hijaz passed through Najd, which brought in some outside influences, but when the power of the caliphs declined, the caravan route between Baghdad and Mecca that had passed through Najd fell into disuse. By 1300 very few caravans passed through Najd and the people of Najd lived for centuries with very little contact with other people. The Hijaz, on the other hand, had abundant, regular exposure to the outside world through contact with traders and pilgrims from all over. These different levels of exposure to outside influences caused the Hijaz and Najd to develop into essentially two different Arabias. In the west the Hijaz took on a more worldly and tolerant quality in light of foreign traffic that moved through it, while in the central and eastern part of the peninsula, Najd remained an isolated stronghold of strict religious views. This religious climate prepared Najd for the Wahhabi Islam that took root there in the eighteenth century. It was in the harsh environment, physically and spiritually, that the Al Saud clan came to power in Najd.

THE AL SAUD FAMILY AND WAHHABI ISLAM, 1500–1850

The Al Saud clan originated in Ad Diriyah in the center of Najd, close to the modern capital of Riyadh. Ancestors of the Al Saud family settled there, and over time developed the area into a small town where the clan that would become the Al Saud became the recognized leaders.

The rise of the Al Saud clan would probably not have been possible without the help of a Muslim scholar named Muhammad Ibn Abd Al Wahhab. He grew up in Uyaynah, an oasis in southern Najd, where he studied the strictest form of Muslim law. In the early eighteenth century, he left Uyaynah to study with other religion teachers in Medina, Iraq, and

Iran, gradually formulating the ideas that were to become the basis of the form of Islam practiced in Saudi Arabia today.

At the beginning of the eighteenth century some forms of Islam, including the Shia sect, were beginning to return to some of the earlier pagan practices that Muhammad had opposed during his life. These beliefs were particularly disturbing to Al Wahhab, so in 1738 he began to write and preach against the Shia sect and in particular its pagan practices. He focused on the Muslim principle that there is only one God, and that God does not share his power with anyone, including leaders of the Shia sect. His preaching frequently offended the members of the Shia sect, who responded by calling Al Wahhab and his followers "Wahhabis," which they considered a derogatory term.

Al Wahhab believed that the central Islamic belief in one God should infuse every aspect of life, including government. Accordingly, he thought Arabian leaders should use their influence and military strength to promote what he considered to be the purist form of Islamic thinking. He also expanded his preaching of Muhammad's fundamental revelation of one God to include strict adherence to the principles of Islamic law, laws that should be enforced by the government as well as by religious leaders. He referred to himself as a "reformer" and began looking for a political figure who might help him spread his ideas to a wider audience.

Disturbed by the resurgence of pagan beliefs in some forms of Islam, Al Wahhab began to write and preach that there was only one God.

Shia leaders in Al Hufuf were understandably alarmed by the anti-Shia tone of the Wahhabi message. Partly as a result of their influence, Al Wahhab was forced to leave eastern Najd. He traveled to Ad Diriyah, where he had earlier made contact with Muhammad Ibn Saud, the town's leader at the time. When Al Wahhab arrived in Ad Diriyah, the Al Saud clan was ready to support him. In 1744 the Al Sauds and Al Wahhab swore an oath to work together to establish a state run according to strict Islamic principles. Prior to that agreement the Al Saud clan had been

conventional tribal leaders. This new pact between the Al Sauds and Al Wahhab and their followers gave the Al Saud clan a deeper authority and power.

The clearly defined religious mission that Al Wahhab offered the receptive Al Saud clan became the defining element of the clan's leadership and political authority. The Wahhabi sense of religious purpose remains the core of political thought in Saudi Arabia today.

Driven by his new religious mission, the leader of the Al Saud clan, Muhammad Ibn Saud, led his army into the towns and villages of Najd intent on eradicating the pagan Shia practices. Beyond this religious purpose, these military actions resulted in bringing most of the tribes and settlements of Najd into a loose federation headed by the Al Saud clan. By 1765 Muhammad Ibn Saud's forces had established Wahhabism as the predominant form of Islam and the Al Saud clan as the political authority over most of Najd.

After Muhammad Ibn Saud died in 1765, his son, Abd al Aziz, took his armies west to spread the Wahhabi creed into the Hijaz, which was by then ruled by the Turkish sultan in Istanbul, the capital of the Ottoman Empire. By 1803 the Al Saud armies were attacking pagan or Shia populations everywhere; they even attacked Mecca and Medina, where the Shia were a minority. The Al Sauds focused on destroying every Shia structure that had anything to do with polytheistic rituals, a rampage that repeated Muhammad's destruction of pagan idols when he reentered Mecca in 628.

If the Al Saud clan had remained in Najd, most of the rest of the world would never have heard of them, but attacking the Hijaz brought the Al Sauds into conflict with the larger Islamic world. The Shia practices that the Wahhabis attempted to destroy were still important to other Muslim sects, including the Ottoman Turks, who controlled not only the Hijaz but also most of the Islamic empire at the time. The powerful Ottomans and many other Muslims were enraged by Wahhabi destruction of shrines and restricted access to holy cities by the upstart Al Sauds.

By the nineteenth century, however, the Ottomans had been weakened by wars on other fronts and lacked the forces to reclaim the Hijaz. They sent one of their ambitious allies, Muhammad Ali, the semi-independent commander of the Ottoman outpost in Egypt, to recapture the Hijaz.

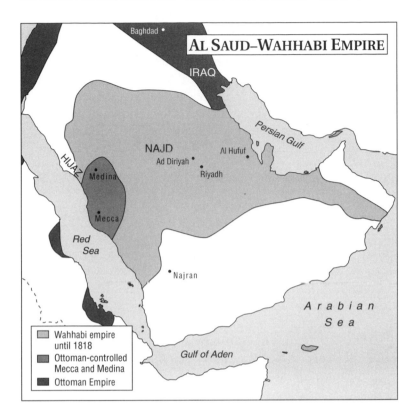

Muhammad Ali and his son, Tursun, easily defeated Al Saud's forces at Mecca and Medina, and forced them to retreat to Najd. Muhammad Ali pursued them. The Al Sauds made their stand at their traditional capital of Ad Diriyah, where they managed to hold out for two years against the superior Egyptian forces. In the end, however, the Al Sauds proved no match for the more modern army of the Egyptians, and Ad Diriyah fell in 1818.

NINETEENTH-CENTURY ARABIA

After his military victories over the Al Saud clan, Muhammad Ali sought to strengthen his control over the Arabian Peninsula by removing all members of the clan from the area. Al Wahhab and Al Saud had since died and the new leader of the Al Saud clan, Abd Allah, was captured and beheaded. Muhammad Ali destroyed the Al Saud capital city of Ad Diriyah and sent troops to strategic parts of Arabia to maintain control. The surviving members of the family left the country or went into hiding.

One of those who escaped, Turki ibn Abd Allah, hid for two years among loyal forces in the south of the peninsula. After a few unsuccessful attempts Turki managed to recapture Ad Diriyah in 1821, and from its ruins he began to rebuild the Al Saud attack force. Soon he had a strong enough army to recapture Riyadh in Najd. Then from Riyadh, Turki led the Al Saud forces as they recaptured the rest of Najd in 1824. Turki was able to retake Najd so quickly because the Al Sauds and Wahhabis who had controlled the area for fifty years had instilled a deep loyalty to the Al Saud clan and to Wahhabi religious principles.

From their base in Riyadh, Turki and his successors ruled the region to the north and south of Najd and continued to spread their influence until Wahhabism was well established along most of the Arabian coast of the Persian Gulf. At this point the Al Saud realm was less a unified country than a loose federation held together by a combination of treaties and local leaders who shared a common adherence to the strict Muslim beliefs of Wahhabism. This confederation was a first for desert tribes that had been fighting each other for generations at great cost in energy and resources.

THE AL SAUD POWER BASE

Although rival clans within the region and foreigners from as far away as England would control much of the Arabian Peninsula in the years to come, the Al Sauds continued to enjoy a fierce loyalty among the desert nomads. Ultimately, the Al Saud clan would reassert its ambition to rule the Arabian Peninsula.

The Ascent of Modern Saudi Arabia

The founding of the modern state of Saudi Arabia and its spectacular rise from a tribal desert society to a wealthy and internationally influential kingdom took place because of the vision, courage, will power, and faith of one man, Ibn Saud bin Abdul Rahman Al Saud. Known simply as Ibn Saud, he united the scattered and warring tribes of the peninsula, drove the foreigners from Arabian soil and conquered all rivals, founded the kingdom of Saudi Arabia, and used the new wealth from oil to put the country on a path toward modernization.

The Rise of Ibn Saud

As the second decade of the twentieth century began, the Al Saud clan had been driven out of their traditional homeland in the central Arabian region of Najd by the armies of the Rashidi clan. Most of the remaining Al Sauds were living in exile in the small kingdom of Kuwait at the northern end of the Persian Gulf. As a result, Ibn Saud lived most of his early life in Kuwait. In the end Ibn Saud succeeded in recovering the territory once controlled by the Al Saud clan and expanded it into a kingdom founded on the religious fervor of Wahhabi Islam.

In 1902, when he was only twenty years old, Ibn Saud began his campaign to regain his clan's homeland. That year he led a small group of warriors in a bold surprise attack on the heavily fortified headquarters of the Rashidi clan, who controlled Riyadh. Though greatly outnumbered, Ibn Saud and his men defeated the Rashidis and recaptured Riyadh. The defeat of the Rashidis represented a major victory for Ibn Saud and established him as the legitimate leader of the Al Saud clan, gaining the support of the Wahhabi leaders and other tribes and clans throughout Arabia.

Ibn Saud regained his homeland by leading a group of Al Saud warriors to victory over the Rashidis and Ottoman Turks.

Though important, the defeat of the Rashidis was only one of Ibn Saud's goals. He needed to purge Arabia of the Ottoman Turks, who controlled much of the peninsula at the time, without allowing the British an opportunity to grab power. Fortunately for the Al Sauds, the Turks' military position was its weakest in a century. When Ibn Saud took his army to the oasis town of Al Hufuf, the center of Ottoman control in eastern Arabia, he was able to beat the Turks in a battle that was the turning point in his efforts to drive them out of all of eastern Arabia. Soon the Ottoman governor in Iraq formally relinquished control of the eastern part of the Arabian Peninsula to Ibn Saud.

With the area from Riyadh east to the Persian Gulf under his control, Ibn Saud had taken the first steps in creating the kingdom of Saudi Arabia. In the west, however, rival clans still held control. Ibn Saud knew he would need a larger army to deal with the west, and he found just such an army in the growing Ikhwan movement.

For some time a strict Islamic movement called the Ikhwan was spreading among the nomadic Bedouin of Arabia. Embracing Wahhabi Islam, the members of the Ikhwan were extremely militant about enforcing their orthodox beliefs. Ibn Saud knew the Ikhwan would follow him into battle with the non-Wahhabi clans, especially the Sharif clan, who controlled the Hijaz and other areas in the western part of the peninsula. The situation was complicated, however, by the presence of the British, who sought control of the peninsula for themselves to protect the lines of supply between England and British-controlled India. The British were allied with the Sharif clan, primarily because the Sharifs were fighting the Ottomans, who still exercised control in the Hijaz. Ibn Saud had to somehow overcome the Sharifs, push the

Ottomans out of the Hijaz, and demonstrate to the British that he could control the army and preserve British interests while he formed an independent Saudi Arabia. He was also aware that if he failed to convince the British that he was the right man to rule Arabia, they had enough military power to take over the peninsula themselves.

By 1915 nearly one hundred thousand Ikhwan were waiting in Najd for a chance to fight under Ibn Saud. He knew he had a powerful weapon in the Ikhwan, but one that he had to use very carefully lest in their fanaticism they attack the British as well the Ottomans and Sharifs.

Ibn Saud's choices were limited. His allies, the Ikhwan, harbored a grudge against the Sharifs of Mecca because they were traditional opponents of Wahhabism. The Sharifs had also antagonized the Ikhwan by forbidding them from making the pilgrimage to Mecca, and besides, they had joined with the non-Muslim British in fighting the Muslim Ottomans. Ibn Saud devised a plan that involved a limited attack on the Sharif-controlled Hijaz, removing the power of the Sharifs and attacking the Ottomans, laying the foundation for taking over the Hijaz and forming a new country that reached from the Red Sea to the Persian Gulf.

In 1919 Ibn Saud and his Ikhwan army met the Sharif army in a battle near the the Hijaz-Najd border. The Ikhwan completely destroyed the Sharif army, leaving the Hijaz defenseless in the face of the fierce warriors from Najd. As the entire western part of the peninsula cowered under the threat of further Ikhwan attacks, the British watched closely, undecided how to respond to Ibn Saud and his Ikhwan army. Ibn Saud knew that Mecca and Medina were his for the taking, but he also knew that the British could respond with a major military offensive and possibly take over all of Arabia. He carefully directed the Ikhwan armies toward other areas of the peninsula that were still under the control of non-Wahhabi Arabs. Whenever the Ikhwan army's movements began to threaten British interests, Ibn Saud would step in to restrain the troops.

The Sharif clan was still allied with the British, but they no longer had an army. Ibn Saud decided to leave them in political control of the Hijaz to help him gain the trust and confidence of the British. When World War I ended, Britain's strategic interest in the Hijaz or in supporting the Sharifs waned. Ibn Saud's success at restraining the Ikhwan from

THE ARAB AS SEEN THROUGH THE EYES OF LAWRENCE OF ARABIA

T. E. Lawrence was a British soldier during World War I who served as Great Britain's military adviser to the Arab leaders in the Hijaz, which was under the control of the Ottoman Turks at the time. Turkey was an ally of Germany during World War I, and therefore the Ottomans were enemies of Great Britain. In Arabia, Lawrence became a student of Arab culture and mastered not only the Arabic language but various tribal dialects as well. He was fond of wearing Arab clothes and living like a desert tribesman, behavior that earned him the title "Lawrence of Arabia." Though he became close to many Arab leaders, his ultimate purpose was always to advance the British war effort. As such, his approach to the Arab world was always self-serving and two-faced. Despite this, his observations provided intriguing glimpses into Arab culture.

In Lawrence's dispatches to his commanding officers, he frequently talked about the Arab mind and how the British could manipulate Arabs to serve their own needs. In 1917 he wrote in his book *The Seven Pillars of Wisdom*:

> The foreigner and Christian is not a popular person in Arabia. However friendly and informal the treatment of yourself may be, remember always that your foundations are very sandy ones. . . . [The Arab] conviction of the truth of their faith, and its share in every act and thought and principle of their daily life is so intimate and intense as to be unconscious, unless roused by opposition. Their religion is as much a part of nature to them as is sleep or food. . . . In familiar conditions they fight well, but strange events cause panic. . . . If the objective is a good one (booty) they will attack like fiends, they are splendid scouts. . . . The beginning and ending of the secret of handling Arabs is unremitting study of them. Keep always on your guard; never say an unnecessary thing: watch yourself and your companions all the time: hear all that passes, search out what is going on beneath the surface, read their characters, discover their tastes and their weaknesses and keep everything you find out to yourself.

T. E. Lawrence, a military adviser to the Arab leaders in the Hijaz during World War I, was nicknamed "Lawrence of Arabia."

attacking British interests had also earned him the respect of the British. At last the time was right to move on the Hijaz. Although the British did not encourage Ibn Saud to attack Mecca and Medina and the rest of the Hijaz, they made it clear they would not oppose him, either. In 1924 the Ikhwan armies under Ibn Saud took over the Hijaz with little opposition from the Sharifs or anyone else.

The capture of the Hijaz was a great victory, but it complicated Ibn Saud's rule. He was at heart a traditional Arab clan leader who had earned the loyalty of various tribes because of his remarkable military successes. But Ibn Saud was also a Wahhabi religious leader who enjoyed the intense loyalty of the Ikhwan. As the new ruler of Mecca and Medina, Ibn Saud now had custodial responsibility over the two shrines most important to all Muslims, not just the Ikhwan. Therefore Ibn Saud had to restrain the more fanatical of his Wahhabi followers, particularly the Ikhwan, while working to win the support of the extremely influential local religious authorities in the Hijaz.

Ibn Saud knew that if he was to build a peninsula-wide nation, he had to be fair to all Muslims living there, not just the Wahhabis. This infuriated the Ikhwan. The Ikhwan and other ultraorthodox Wahhabis were also opposed to modern machines, particularly those used for communication like the telegraph, and to the increasing presence of non-Muslim foreigners in Arabia. They also continued to object to many of the practices of non-Wahhabi Muslims. Soon the Ikhwan, always ready to force their message on anyone who did not accept it, resumed attacks on non-Wahhabi Muslims and even Wahhabis who were not sufficiently strict in their observance of Islamic law. In some cases they crossed borders established by the British after World War I in defiance of Ibn Saud's authority.

Finally Ibn Saud was forced to fight his old allies, the Ikhwan. He raised an army in the traditional Arabian way, by going out into the country and presenting his case to potential fighters and to the local religious committees called ulama. By the force of his personality and the respect accorded his pure Al Saud lineage, Ibn Saud succeeded in raising a new army. After attempting unsuccessfully to deal with the Ikhwan in nonmilitary ways, in 1929 Ibn Saud met and defeated the main Ikhwan army. Some Ikhwan remained loyal to Ibn Saud and eventually formed the core of the new kingdom's national guard.

IBN SAUD'S TERRITORY

SYRIA

IRAQ

IRAN

TRANS-
JORDAN

HIJAZ

Persian Gulf

NAJD

Al Hufuf

Medina

Riyadh

Mecca

Red
Sea

Arabian
Sea

Extent of Ibn Saud's territory:
■ 1912   ■ 1920   ■ 1925
▨ Sharif of Mecca and Medina

THE FOUNDING OF MODERN SAUDI ARABIA AND THE RULE OF IBN SAUD

Once the fanatical and fearsome Ikhwan had been defeated, the majority of Arabia's leaders supported Ibn Saud as their king. With all obstacles removed and with the support of all the major clans of Arabia, in 1932 Ibn Saud formally founded the kingdom of Saudi Arabia.

From the start Ibn Saud did not rule alone, but relied on the advice and approval of the powerful group of religious leaders known as the ulama. When the ulama disagreed with him, rather than simply overrule them, he worked hard to change their opinions. For example, when he wanted to build a modern radio communications system in Arabia, the ultraconservative ulama opposed it on the basis that radio did not exist in the time of Muhammad. Ibn Saud recognized the importance of radio, so he set up a demonstration showing that the holy book of Islam, the Quran, could be broadcast by radio. Reconsidering, the ulama gave radio their approval.

Ibn Saud was always careful to avoid making enemies, and he tried to turn enemies into allies. He especially focused on smoothing old rivalries. For example, he arranged the marriages of three Rashidi widows with men from his own family, and he gave members of the Sharif family large tracts of land.

But he was often frustrated in his attempts to follow the tribal tradition of rewarding the loyalty of allies by granting them special favors and gifts because the new kingdom had little money. Najd had never been particularly prosperous, and the Hijaz, while somewhat richer because of income from pilgrims, was hit hard by the worldwide economic depression that followed the great stock market crash of 1929. Consequently, Ibn Saud could provide little in the way of traditional favors and almost nothing in the way of government services. That was all to change very soon.

THE OIL-RICH KINGDOM

Oil was first found in Arabia before World War I, but not until the early 1930s, after an American company won the rights to develop that oil, did the world learn the true extent of the fabulous riches that waited beneath the sands of Saudi Arabia. By 1938, Standard Oil of California had discovered several enormous deposits of oil and gas beneath the gravelly surface of the desert near the Persian Gulf coast. New discoveries followed. Oil flowed from wells in the seabed of the Persian Gulf, the coastal plains of eastern Arabia, and the Empty Quarter, where the world's largest oil deposit was found.

The discovery of oil did not bring immediate wealth to Saudi Arabia. The country's economy did not begin its dramatic improvement until Saudi Arabia and other oil-producing nations raised oil prices in the 1970s. Then spectacular amounts of money began flowing into the kingdom, creating a large financial surplus. Saudi Arabia's rulers vowed to use their new riches for two primary purposes: to modernize the nation and to assist other Islamic Arab populations.

But then in 1982, and again in 1986 when oil-producing nations outside the Middle East raised their oil production, oil prices dropped sharply. The government of Saudi Arabia went from managing a cash surplus to coping with growing shortages. Because the government had committed large sums of money to a variety of projects, it was forced to

A lone derrick pumps oil in a desert of Saudi Arabia, the world's largest oil producer.

sell foreign assets and borrow money. When the price of oil recovered in 1990, Saudi Arabia, more cautious this time, resumed a variety of projects designed to improve the quality of life for its citizens and to strengthen the military power of the country and its allies.

As 2000 dawned, Saudi Arabia was the world's largest oil producer, pumping about 13 percent of the total world output. The kingdom was very close to being a one-product economy as oil accounted for between 70 and 80 percent of the country's income and 90 percent of its exports.

THE SECOND KING OF SAUDI ARABIA

Ibn Saud dedicated his final years to modernizing Saudi Arabia. By the time of his death in 1953, the kingdom was beginning to enjoy the fruits of his labor with new roads, basic communication networks, power plants, water systems, and improvements in education, health care, and agriculture.

When Ibn Saud died, his eldest son, Saud, was crowned the next king of Saudi Arabia. Saud lacked his father's leadership abilities and was not up to the difficult challenges of the next decade. He increased his personal palace guard to the size of a small army and built lavish palaces for himself and his closest allies. Despite growing annual oil revenues, he did little to improve government services to the country's citizens. King Saud's financial mismanagement and extravagant personal spending, along with the lack of new public projects and educational institutions and the low wages paid to the growing labor force, led to rising dissatisfaction among members of the Al Saud family, the ulama, and ordinary citizens.

THE INFLUENTIAL KING FAISAL

The ulama finally had enough of Saud's excesses and shortcomings as a leader. In November 1964 they issued a religious decree that deposed Saud and made Faisal, another of Ibn Saud's sons, king. This action ended almost a decade of external and internal pressure to depose Saud.

Faisal was a deeply religious man and a strong leader who was committed to the gradual modernization of his country. Faisal's rule was characterized by his respect for Arabian tradition and Islamic morality. He believed that leadership was an extension of his religious devotion and as such it demanded thoughtfulness, dignity, and integrity. His traditionalism and religious idealism, in a country populated by traditional and religious people, heightened his effectiveness as a politician, economist, and leader of his country.

King Faisal committed himself to the gradual modernization of Saudi Arabia.

Whereas Saud had generally cut himself off from the citizens of Saudi Arabia during his reign, King Faisal made himself available to the public through the Arabian tribal tradition of open meetings called majlis. Like Saudi kings before and after him, Faisal depended on the majlis to become familiar with the needs of his people.

Faisal, like his father, was intent on bringing technology to Saudi Arabia, always mindful of those who opposed modernization. He believed Saudi Arabia could benefit from technology while retaining its allegiance to Islam. But Ibn Saud's path was difficult to follow.

In 1965, as the first Saudi Arabian television broadcasts were offending ultraconservative elements in the country, one of Faisal's own nephews headed an attack on a new television station and was killed in a shootout with the police. This family tragedy did not, however, cause Faisal to

THE ROYAL DIWAN

The executive office of the king of Saudi Arabia is the Royal Diwan, located in the capital city of Riyadh. The king's private office is here, as are the offices of his principle advisers for domestic politics, religious affairs, and international relations. The king conducts most routine affairs of government in the Royal Diwan.

In addition to the king and his immediate advisers, the heads of several government departments have their offices in the Royal Diwan. These include the Chief of Protocol; the Office of Bedouin Affairs; the Department of Religious Research, Missionary Activities; and Guidance; and the Committees for the Propagation of Virtue and Prevention of Vice (popularly known as the Committees for Public Morality). The Department of Religious Research, Missionary Activities, and Guidance, headed by the most senior of the ulama, is also here.

The king also holds his regular majlis, or court, in the Royal Diwan. The majlis provides Saudi Arabian citizens an opportunity to make personal appeals to the king regarding local problems or request assistance in private matters. Typically a person comes to the majlis seeking the king's intervention with the governmental bureaucracy. The citizen explains the problem or need and presents a written petition. Then the king studies the written petition and answers it at a later majlis.

withdraw his support for the television project or to change his slow but steady pace of modernization.

In more than ten years as king, Faisal devoted himself to maintaining this balance between progressive and conservative values. This balancing act was carried out with such wisdom and respect for all people that he gained recognition among world leaders. In 1975 Faisal was named *Time* magazine's "Man of the Year." The magazine described him as one of the world's most powerful men because of the oil wealth he controlled and one of its most respected leaders based on his calm style of leadership and his efforts on behalf of peace in the Middle East.

Faisal's popularity abroad, however, did little toward solving his problems at home. Egypt had been antagonistic toward Saudi Arabia's monarchy for years, and when a long-simmering uprising in the southwestern part of the country along the border with Yemen turned into a full-fledged rebellion in 1962, Egypt decided to back the rebels. As the rebellion dragged on, Egyptian aircraft bombed military installations and towns in southern Saudi Arabia and Egyptian terrorists attacked members of the royal family and foreigners working in Saudi Arabia. The likelihood of all-out war between Saudi Arabia and Egypt increased with every attack. The situation was made more tense when deposed king Saud, living in Egypt and hoping for a chance to return to power in Saudi Arabia, made a personal gift of $1 million to the rebels. Attacks continued and tensions simmered for five years until the Arab-Israeli War of 1967 brought an end to hostilities when the two countries set aside their differences in the face of a common enemy, Israel.

That war resulted in the defeat of Egyptian, Jordanian, and Syrian forces and Israeli occupation of parts of Syria and Jordan, including Jerusalem, a city sacred to both Muslims and Jews. Following the 1967 war, Faisal showed that he was serious about pan-Arab cooperation when Saudi Arabia, along with Libya and Kuwait, established an immense fund to help the countries that had suffered most from the war, especially Egypt and Jordan. Saudi Arabia contributed $140 million, an act that convinced Egypt to finally stop backing the rebellion in southwest Saudi Arabia.

Faisal also led Arab nations in demanding the removal of Israeli forces from Arab lands captured during the 1967 war.

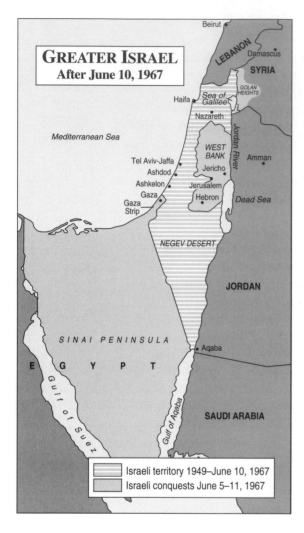

Israel's steadfast refusal to give up the Arab territory it had seized during the brief war led Faisal to use his most effective weapon: oil. He tried to persuade the United States to withdraw its support for Israel by threatening to reduce oil deliveries. Finally, in October 1973, he made good on his threat when another war broke out between Israel and two Arab states. Prodded by Faisal, the Organization of Petroleum Exporting Countries (OPEC) raised oil prices and ceased oil shipments to any country considered a supporter of Israel. The goal of the oil embargo was to pressure supporters of Israel into forcing Israel to withdraw from occupied Arab territory. Though the embargo did not achieve its goal, it resulted in a tripling of oil prices, which increased Saudi Arabia's income dramatically.

Taking advantage of the kingdom's revenue windfall, Faisal started a number of ambitious projects to further improve health care, education, and communications in Saudi Arabia. His efforts were cut short in 1975 when an assassin, his own nephew and the brother of the man killed in the 1965 television station incident, shot and killed him. Saudi Arabia mourned Faisal's passing, calling him the greatest king since Ibn Saud.

ANOTHER OF IBN SAUD'S SONS BECOMES KING

Following Faisal's assassination, Prince Khalid, another son of Ibn Saud, was immediately crowned king. As king, Khalid soon found himself facing the greatest challenges the young kingdom had faced since its inception.

In 1979 Egypt signed a peace treaty with Israel and the world watched to see how Khalid would handle this new development in Arab-Israeli relations. Khalid announced that he considered the treaty between Egypt and Israel a betrayal of Arab unity. He immediately broke diplomatic relations with Egypt and led the Arab world in placing economic sanctions against Egypt.

Consumed by international events, Khalid failed to attend to long-simmering resentment regarding Saudi Arabia's modernization programs. Then in November 1979, he was jolted back to domestic concerns when about five hundred armed dissidents, passionate opponents of the modernization of Saudi Arabia, invaded and seized the most holy sanctuary of Islam, the Grand Mosque in Mecca. The seizure presented a problem of unprecedented proportions for Saudi leaders. They opposed the seizure as a terrorist act, yet felt a good deal of sympathy with the dissidents' politics. Many of the people who had seized the Grand Mosque came from highly respected tribes that were traditionally loyal to the Al Saud clan; Khalid himself had spent much time in the desert with many of these tribes. Not knowing how to respond, Saudi leaders at first expressed shock but took no action. Finally the decision

King Khalid declared that the 1979 peace treaty Egypt signed with Israel was a betrayal of Arab unity.

was made to send in the military and retake the mosque. First, however, the king had to get permission from the ulama because weapons and bloodshed are forbidden in Islam's most holy shrine. The ulama granted a special exception and the Saudi military ended the takeover, but at a cost of dozens of lives of both dissidents and soldiers. The surviving dissidents were captured, tried for treason and other crimes, found guilty, and publicly executed.

The tension between those who wished to modernize Saudi Arabia and those who opposed modernization surfaced again just two weeks after the siege of the Grand Mosque. Religious riots broke out in eastern Saudi Arabia with many rioters carrying posters of Ayatollah Khomeini, Iran's fundamentalist Muslim leader. Khomeini called for a return to strict Islamic practices and condemnation of Western values, and Muslims in many lands heeded his call. It took nearly twenty-thousand national guard troops to quell the riots; many demonstrators were killed and hundreds more were arrested.

THE REIGN OF KING FAHD

In June 1982, after years of failing health, Khalid died. The new king, Fahd, yet another son of Ibn Saud, vowed to continue the domestic development and improvements in social services begun by Faisal. He also undertook a program to expand services and safety for the millions of pilgrims coming to Mecca every year. This included increasing the capac-

THE ULAMA: FATWAS AND RELIGION IN THE SAUDI ARABIAN GOVERNMENT

The ulama, as Saudi Arabia's top-level Islamic religious leaders and teachers are called, have played an important role in the kingdom since Ibn Saud's earliest victories. Except for Iran, Saudi Arabia is the only Muslim country where the ulama are an open political force. The kingdom's ulama include religious scholars, judges, lawyers, seminary teachers, and prayer leaders. Of the approximately ten thousand ulama in Saudi Arabia, only thirty or forty of the most senior scholars, comprising the Council of Senior Ulama, have true political power. Normally this council meets with the king weekly, more frequently during emergencies because most of the king's decisions have religious implications that require the advice or approval of the ulama. For example, in 1979 the Council of Senior Ulama signed the religious edict (called a fatwa) that allowed the use of military force to overcome the armed dissidents who had occupied the Grand Mosque in Mecca. Then when Iraq's Saddam Hussein invaded Kuwait in 1990 and the United States wanted to bring military forces and aircraft into the northeastern part of Saudi Arabia, many devout Muslims feared that the presence of so many non-Muslims on Saudi soil would violate the sanctity of the holy land. King Fahd defused these concerns by obtaining approval for the foreign military presence from the Council of Senior Ulama.

Most of the Saudi Arabian ulama belong to the large Al ash Shaykh family, which are descended from the founder of Wahhabi Islam; these ulama, with close ties to the royal family, can usually be counted on to side with the king. Ulama from other families, however, tend to be more critical of the king and senior ulama. In 1992 a group of these ulama sent a public letter to King Fahd criticizing him personally. This unprecedented act caused a major reaction throughout Saudi Arabia and so infuriated Fahd that he dismissed a number of influential ulama.

ity of the Grand Mosque, which now holds in excess of a million worshipers at one time.

In November 1987, Fahd reestablished diplomatic relations between Egypt and Saudi Arabia. When he visited Egypt in 1989, he received a huge welcome on the streets of Cairo in appreciation of his having paved the way for Egypt to return to the family of Arab states.

During the 1990s Fahd concentrated on diversifying Saudi Arabia's economic base with the goal of making the country less dependent on oil income. Encouraged by Fahd's policies, many private companies began to enter the oil industry, which had primarily been run by the government. As a result, by the year 2000, private industry in Saudi Arabia accounted for more than a third of the country's income.

CONCLUSION

Ibn Saud, the founder and first king of Saudi Arabia, was survived by thirty sons, four of whom have become king. Saudi Arabia's monarchy, from Ibn Saud to Fahd, has ruled by virtue of his position in the Al Saud clan. The king must seek the approval of the ulama, the country's religious leaders, for many decisions because he is personally responsible for protecting Islam's most holy shrines. While the monarchy has been the primary shaper of Saudi Arabia's destiny since the country came into existence, its influence has been moderated by the influx of Western and non-Muslim people, thought, and technology that has accompanied the country's great oil wealth.

4 Daily Life in Saudi Arabia

During the second half of the twentieth century, Saudi Arabia experienced a dramatic transformation from a mostly rural and nomadic society to a predominantly urban one. With urbanization has come new ideas, introduced by an influx of outsiders and, increasingly, by Saudis themselves. Despite strong winds of change blowing in the kingdom of Saudi Arabia, it is still a remarkably traditional society in which deeply held Islamic values shape almost every aspect of daily life.

As in the past, Saudi Arabians today are divided between the desire for modernization and the desire to preserve traditional Islamic values. This tension has produced some unusual practices, such as the Saudi government's official policy of insulating the Muslim population from the influences of the foreign community. In most parts of the country, foreigners are strongly encouraged to live in their own compounds, particularly in the oil communities where many of the engineers are American or European. But not all the pressure for change comes from foreigners. In a country where tribal traditions, unchanged for more than a millennium, determine public policy and law, the call for change is heard more and more frequently.

In an effort to combat these voices for change, the government practices strict censorship, designed to restrict public access to any thought that contradicts Islamic teachings. In Saudi Arabia, censorship of newspapers, magazines, books, television, movies, and the Internet has been and continues to be standard policy. Nevertheless, traditional Islamic and tribal values have been weakened by challenges from educated young Saudis who have adopted different values from the preceding generation, including a desire for a more active role in government, less absolute power in the hands of the king, and less power in the hands of the ulama.

Nevertheless, the fact remains that the populace of Saudi Arabia is unanimous in the belief that modernization, in whatever form, must continue to reflect Islamic values. Today Afghanistan is the only country in the world that comes close to incorporating religion into daily life to the extent that Saudi Arabia does.

ISLAM: THE CORE OF SAUDI ARABIAN LIFE

The alliance between the Wahhabi religious reformers and the Al Saud clan provided the compelling focus needed to unite what had previously been a fragmented and bickering tribal society. Wahhabi Islam continues to be the foundation of almost all aspects of Saudi society. Islam is the only officially recognized religion of Saudi Arabia.

Wahhabi Muslims take the basic duties of Islam very seriously, solemn duties that are spelled out in "the five pillars of Islam." These five mandatory duties, the true backbone of every Muslim society, are: formally affirming faith in Muhammad's teachings, reciting prayers five times every day, giving charitably, fasting during the Islamic month of Ramadan, and making a pilgrimage to Mecca. Furthermore, Muslims must perform these acts of worship with a conscious intent, not out of habit.

Five times every day—at dawn, midday, midafternoon, sunset, and nightfall—the devout Saudi Arabian turns to face Mecca and prays. Whenever possible, Muslim men pray in congregation under the guidance of a prayer leader at a mosque, the Islamic place of worship. On Fridays, praying at a mosque is required. Women usually pray at home but may also attend public worship at a mosque, although they must be segregated from the men. At the appropriate five times each day, the community is called to prayer by the voice of the muezzin, which emanates from the towerlike minarets that are the landmark of every mosque.

In the early days of Islam, religious authorities imposed a tax on personal property that reflected a person's wealth. The income from this tax was distributed to the mosques and the needy. Gradually this practice changed from a mandatory tax to voluntary charitable contributions to the needy. Today it is the duty of all Muslims to be charitable.

The entire ninth month of the Muslim calendar, named Ramadan, is a time of mandatory fasting. This fast honors

CHANGING TIMES: INTERNET FOR SAUDI ARABIAN WOMEN

From most outward signs, life for women in Saudi Arabia is much as it was a thousand years ago. In public, women must wear abayas, voluminous, flowing black robes that cover the wearer from head to toe except for the hands and face. Women are still prohibited from driving a motor vehicle, traveling alone, attending classes with men, or even mixing with men who are not members of their immediate families. Most women abide by these Islamic traditions and laws, but that does not mean they lack curiosity about the outside world. The possibilities for a Saudi woman to learn about life beyond the kingdom or to actually communicate with people in the West have been very limited—that is, until the development of the Internet.

The Saudi Arabian government finally allowed Internet providers to do business in the kingdom in July 1999. Before that, tens of thousands of Saudi citizens dialed long-distance providers in the United States and other countries to log on to the Internet. When the Saudi government finally realized that it was impossible to enforce the prohibition on Internet access, they decided to allow Internet service providers to begin operating in the kingdom as long as they accept government censorship of all content that is political, sexual, or critical of the Saudi monarchy. Now computers in the kingdom are humming with web surfers, and there are dozens of new Internet service providers. It is very common in Saudi Arabia to have "ladies only" banks, schools, and shops, and Saudi Internet sites offer special "ladies only" channels.

AwalNet for Ladies is an example of an Internet provider designed specifically for Saudi Arabian women that provides a broad new gateway to the outer world. On this site technical support is even staffed by women, since many Saudi females are unaccustomed to dealing with men. Previously isolated from most of the events and resources of the world, today's

Muhammad's receipt of God's revelations, revelations that compose the primary book of Islamic Scripture, the Quran. Muslims believe that fasting is an act of self-discipline that leads to piety and expresses submission and commitment to God. A sacrifice required of rich and poor alike, fasting un-derscores the equality of all Muslims and strengthens their

Saudi Arabian woman can go online for international news, research, job hunting, health care and fitness information, movie and book reviews, education, shopping, finding child care, following fashion trends, and reading the latest Islamic news.

The Saudi government and various religious and education authorities are, however, concerned about the threat to Islamic values posed by the Internet. At a prominent girl's school, for instance, administrators have prohibited use of the Internet on school computers for fear of what the girls might be writing and reading in various chat rooms. At the AwalNet office, staffers tell young women to be sure to remain anonymous if they log onto chat rooms to protect themselves from recriminations from the Saudi Arabian religious police.

For the Saudi Arabian female who has traditionally spent long hours isolated at home, Internet services like AwalNet for Ladies are a breath of fresh air and an opportunity for social change.

Saudi Arabian women now have access to the abundance of information that can be found on the Internet.

sense of community. During Ramadan every Muslim must fast, with the exception of sick or weak people, pregnant or nursing women, soldiers on duty, travelers on necessary journeys, and young children. Fasting Muslims may not eat, drink, or smoke anything whatsoever during the daylight hours. The workday is often shortened during this period,

A devout Muslim prostrates himself in prayer.

and some businesses close for all or part of the day. Because the Islamic calendar is based on the lunar month, the Muslim year is eleven days shorter than the solar year. For this reason Ramadan occurs in different seasons over the years. Since fasting involves abstaining even from drinking water, when Ramadan falls in the hot summer, Muslims who do physically taxing work endure considerable hardship. Fasting ends each day at darkness. The month of Ramadan concludes with Id al Fitr, a three-day feast and holiday that is an occasion for much visiting and merriment between family and friends.

The fifth pillar of Islam requires all Muslims, if possible at least once in their lifetime, to make a special pilgrimage, called the hajj, to the holy city of Mecca during the twelfth month of the Islamic calendar.

Besides performing the five basic duties of Islam, Muslims, especially Wahhabi Muslims, believe they have a duty to spread the teachings of Muhammad. This duty is called jihad in Arabic. The word is sometimes translated as "holy war," but most Muslims view this duty as simply a call to civil and personal action to spread the faith.

Daily life in Saudi Arabia embodies more of Islam than just the required basic duties of the faith. Like most other religions, Islam imposes a code of ethical conduct that encourages generosity, fairness, honesty, and respect, and it guides believers in proper family relations. Islamic law, which is the foundation of civil law in Saudi Arabia, specifically forbids adultery, gambling, charging high interest rates on loans, drinking alcohol, and eating pork, blood, or carrion.

Because of the influence of Islam, any expression of class or status is discouraged. Even the king dresses like an ordinary citizen. Of course, there are more or less subtle ways, like the car one drives or the jewelry one wears, to indicate a person's wealth, but Islam stresses that all people are equal in God's eyes. Saudi Arabians are more likely to judge a person on their tribal ties than on their social standing, education, or wealth.

STANDARD OF LIVING

Saudi Arabia remains a divided society. The kingdom displays most of the characteristics of a highly developed nation, yet about a quarter of the population still live in rural areas distant from urban centers. Reflecting the society at large, many rural families are divided. The men often move

All devout Muslims aspire to make a pilgrimage to the holy city of Mecca before they die.

MECCA AND THE HAJJ

For many devout Muslims, making a pilgrimage (called the hajj) to western Saudi Arabia to visit Islam's most holy sites is not only a religious duty but the high point of their spiritual lives as well. During the hajj, the pilgrims form a human river of all races, cultures, and stations in life flowing into western Saudi Arabia.

Mecca is more than a city to Muslims; it is a sanctuary where violence to people, animals, and even plants is prohibited. Mecca is so holy that non-Muslims are not permitted and a special highway diverts non-Muslims around the city.

Improvements in transportation and accommodations have led to a dramatic increase in the number of pilgrims visiting Saudi Arabia on the hajj. In 1965 about 300,000 Muslim pilgrims entered Saudi Arabia. By 1983 that number had climbed to over a million, in 1998 to over two million. In addition to those coming from abroad, nearly a million people living in the kingdom also join in the hajj rituals. A special branch of the Saudi Arabian government handles the complex challenge of accommodating all these visitors from many different countries. Special pilgrimage visas allow each pilgrim to visit Mecca and to make a side trip to Medina to visit Muhammad's tomb. Thousands of trained specialists assist the hajjis, as the pilgrims are called, instructing them in the proper ways to perform the rituals and helping them with the practical matters of their visit.

Since any disturbance could quickly become a disaster when several million pilgrims are involved, the Saudi government has invested heavily in security and facilities for handling the huge numbers of hajjis, but catastrophic incidents have nevertheless drawn the world's attention. A clash in 1987 between demonstrating Iranian pilgrims and Saudi police left 400 people dead. In 1990 pilgrims passing through an overcrowded and poorly ventilated tunnel panicked and 1,426 of them suffocated or were crushed to death.

The hajj continues for nine days, enough time to perform a variety of rituals and to visit the places where the most important events in Muhammad's life took place. The focus of the pilgrimage is Mecca's Grand Mosque, where the Ka'aba is located. The Ka'aba is a cube-shaped sanctuary draped in black cloth that was built, according to Islamic tradition, by Abraham and his son Ismail. The Ka'aba contains a black stone that Muslims believe was given to Abraham by the angel Gabriel. The Ka'aba was a pilgrimage destination even before Islam; according to Islamic tradition, it was cleansed of idols by Muhammad and rededicated to the worship of the one God of Islam.

A tent arises around Mecca during the pilgrimage.

to distant towns to find work as drivers, laborers, or soldiers in the Saudi Arabian National Guard while the women stay behind to raise the children and tend the livestock. Despite the country's wealth, poverty has snared many of Saudi's rural people, and illiteracy, physical distance, and bureaucratic obstacles have limited access to the resources of Saudi Arabia's growing economy.

The majority of Saudi Arabia's citizens enjoy all the trappings of a modern society. Two of the largest and most advanced airports in the world are in Jeddah and Riyadh, where smooth eight-lane highways take the visitor to cities of skyscrapers, modern hotels, luxurious homes, bright signs, shopping malls, and supermarkets. However, other features are rarely found in Western cities. Minarets, the slender towers that are part of every mosque, rise into the desert air from every quarter. Souks, the crowded, traditional markets, retain the boisterous and exciting atmosphere of old Arabia. In the souks, where old-style architecture, meandering passageways, intriguing aromas, and bustling stalls selling spices, gold, and carpets predominate, price tags are only a starting point and bargaining is expected.

Three-quarters of Saudi Arabians live and work in large cities like Riyadh, Jeddah, Yanbu, Medina, Dhahran, and Mecca. Most drive to work in their own cars and work at a wide variety of jobs. They watch television, go to movies and soccer matches, picnic, and in general live lives that are not all that different from urban dwellers anywhere. Most are not rich, but the country's oil wealth makes housing, education, and health care available to all.

Camels, donkey carts, and horses have been replaced by cars; it seems that almost everyone in Saudi Arabia has an automobile. Traffic jams are commonplace, but when the traffic is flowing, driving in Saudi Arabia is an exercise in speed. The speeders are all male because women, whether Saudi or foreign, are prohibited from driving in the kingdom. Drivers routinely whip their cars around as if they are playing soccer with their vehicles. The popular Muslim response to almost any problem is to say "Inshallah!" (translated roughly as the fatalistic "Whatever is God's will!"), and this notion seems to apply to the driving style of most Saudis, as in "If I crash my car and die, Inshallah."

Though most Saudi Arabian families live in modern Western-style houses and apartments, even those that live in traditional housing like these buildings are likely to have modern appliances.

A typical Saudi family is as likely to live in a Western-style apartment as in a traditional Arabic home with a central courtyard and separate women's and men's quarters. Modern appliances, computers, home entertainment centers, and furnishings familiar to an American or European are found in most Saudi homes, although some characteristics of traditional Arab living remain. Many homes, for example, feature low cushions, simple benches, and pillows rather than sofas in the living and sitting rooms, and shoes are usually left at the door.

Throughout Saudi Arabia, ways of life have been changing for several decades as a result of oil wealth and the number of foreigners in the country. Despite all the changes, however, the typical Saudi Arabian retains a deep-rooted love of the traditional way of life based on Islamic and ancient tribal values. In practice this means that prayer, large close-knit families, friendship, communal meals, social separation of men and women, hospitality, and lengthy conversation are the most important aspects of daily living.

WHAT DO SAUDI ARABIANS EAT?

With less than 1 percent total area of the country under cultivation, Saudi Arabia must import most of its food. The government subsidizes some of the cost of these imports and so food is not prohibitively expensive. According to the Saudi government, there is no hunger in the country.

A typical Saudi meal consists of mildly spiced and roasted lamb or chicken served on a bed of seasoned rice with dates and other fruit. The meal is usually eaten while sitting on the floor, using the right hand to form bite-size clumps of food that are tossed into the mouth. Tea or Arabian coffee is served at all meals and at meetings. Camel's milk and yogurt are staple dairy products. In coastal areas many people eat fish, accompanied by rice, salad, and round flat Arabian bread.

Foods from other countries are also popular; in the cities it is not uncommon to find restaurants serving Greek delicacies, burgers, and Japanese dishes within a single block. Their menus will not, however, feature bacon or beer because Muslims are forbidden from eating pork and it is against the law to drink alcohol in Saudi Arabia.

STYLES OF DRESS

Whatever their job or social status, Saudi men almost always wear the traditional thobe, a caftanlike garment that resembles an over-size shirt. To Saudis, the thobe symbolizes the spiritual equality of Muslims; it's loose cut is also perfectly suited to the hot Saudi climate. During hot weather, Saudi men and boys wear white thobes, and during cooler weather, wool thobes in dark colors are common. For important occasions, men wear a bisht over the thobe. The bisht is a long white, brown, or black cloak trimmed in gold embroidery.

The most obvious part of a Saudi Arabian man's headdress is the gutra, a large square of fabric, usually cotton, worn folded into a triangle and centered on the head. Traditionally, Saudis wear either a white or a red-and-white checked gutra. The other two parts of the Saudi male's headdress consist of

GAHWA: ARABIAN COFFEE

Preparing and drinking coffee, called gahwa in Arabic, is a refined tradition in Saudi Arabia. In modern Arabia gahwa is still served with the same ceremony and etiquette used by Bedouin tribes for centuries. According to legend, coffee drinking originated in Arabia almost twelve centuries ago; althought the date has not been proven, most records indicate that the first coffee beans indeed came from the mountains of southwestern Arabia.

The gahwa ritual begins by placing four brass coffeepots next to an open fire. The host roasts the coffee beans over the flame in a shallow, long-handled iron pan. After the roasted beans are cooled, they are placed in a mortar and pulverized with a pestle. As the host pounds the beans in the metal mortar, he creates a musical rhythm listened to by the guests with great appreciation.

The largest of the four coffeepots contains the grounds from previous several days. Water is poured into the second-largest pot, to which the freshly ground coffee is added, and brought to a boil. Then in the mortar the host pulverizes some cardamom seeds, sometimes adding a pinch of saffron, and pours these ground spices into the third coffeepot. This pot is then filled with the freshly brewed coffee from the second pot and brought to a boil again. Finally the coffee is poured into the fourth and smallest pot, ready to serve.

The host will pour himself a small cup first to be sure the taste is right. Then he serves the most important person in the room first. Age takes precedence if there is some doubt as to rank. Until a few years ago men were always served before women, but today that custom is often reversed, particularly if Westerners are among the guests.

Traditionally the cups are only filled halfway, but the guests may have several refills if desired. Politeness dictates accepting only an odd number of cups—one, three, or five—and when a guest has had enough, the empty coffee cup must be jiggled from side to side to indicate that a refill is not desired. To refuse the first round of coffee is considered bad manners and an insult to the host.

Arabian coffee is brewed strong, but it is never sweetened with sugar. Instead, gahwa is traditionally served with fresh dates, which consist of about 50 percent sugar.

the tagia, a small white cap that keeps the gutra from slipping off the head, and the igal, a doubled black cord that holds the gutra in place. Igals range from very simple to very ornate; some men choose not to wear the igal at all.

Most Saudi women appear in public dressed from head to toe in black. Under the voluminous black cloak called an abaya, however, a woman is likely to wear fashionable, colorful garments not much different from women's attire in a typical Western mall. Opinion varies regarding the wearing of the abaya and the veil, but most Saudi women report enjoying the sense of privacy and anonymity that wearing the abaya provides.

The gutra, a large square of fabric, usually cotton, is folded into a triangle and worn on the head of Saudi Arabian men.

GOVERNMENT-SUBSIDIZED HEALTH CARE

Much of the improvement in Saudi Arabia's standard of living is due to the great improvements in health care since the 1970s. Advances in health care over the past few decades have raised the life expectancy at birth to sixty-nine years for males and seventy-three years for females. The major diseases found in Saudi Arabia are malaria, meningitis, bilharzia (a parasitic infection), typhoid, tuberculosis, and lung infections. Compulsory immunization of infants and young children and the introduction in 1986 of an epidemic control system to alert the public to outbreaks of communicable diseases have contributed to the successful eradication of many diseases.

The government of Saudi Arabia has committed vast resources to improving medical care for its citizens, with the goal of providing free medical care for everyone in the kingdom. The number of hospitals and medical personnel have grown steadily for decades until today the ratios of doctors and hospital beds to citizens are about the same as those in the United States.

The King Faisal Medical City near Riyadh is considered one of the most technologically advanced hospital complexes in the world. To provide personnel for the expanding medical facilities, which in the 1990s were staffed largely by foreign physicians, nurses, technicians, and administrators, the government has encouraged medical education in the kingdom and has financed training abroad for promising students to become teachers of medicine. As testament to the government's commitment to improving educational opportunities within the kingdom, four of the kingdom's seven universities now offer medical degrees and operate well-equipped hospitals, and the country has a number of colleges that prepare students for nursing, pharmacology, and other health care professions.

EDUCATION

In Saudi Arabia, education is not compulsory, but it is free. No school in Saudi Arabia, except for some private schools run by and for foreigners, is coeducational. That includes colleges and universities. In the early days of building Saudi's educational system, the nation's leaders believed that men would put the knowledge and skills acquired to

THE ALL-NATURAL TOOTHBRUSH

In any Saudi Arabian town, businessmen, students, merchants, professors, and taxi drivers can be seen chewing publicly on a brown stick several inches long and the diameter of a pencil.

Public tooth hygiene is perfectly acceptable to Saudi Arabians, and the tool they use is the miswak, a natural toothbrush with toothpastelike qualities. This amazing stick, widely used throughout the Arab world, cleans the mouth, whitens the teeth, and sweetens the breath. Muslims use it because Muhammad used it during fasting and advised using it as a breath freshener before prayer. Unlike a conventional plastic toothbrush, the miswak can be used anytime, anywhere, and with no need for toothpaste, vigorous brushing, or spitting.

The miswak comes from the root of the arak tree. Chemical analysis shows that it contains a number of substances that are beneficial to dental health. It has a natural antiseptic that kills harmful bacteria, tannic acid with astringent qualities that protect gums from disease, and aromatic oils that increase salivation. Because of its built-in antiseptic, the miswak needs no cleaning, and because it easily shreds into parallel bristles, it reaches easily between the teeth.

Supermarkets and modern pharmacies in Saudi Arabia do not sell the miswak, so Saudis must seek out special vendors in the souks or in the front of mosques. A new miswak must first be soaked in water to soften the fibers and then the bark at one end is shaved away with a sharp knife. Chewing the shaved end for another minute or so helps to separate the fiber into bristles, and then the miswak is ready. The taste of the miswak is described as slightly bitter.

Does it work? Just look at the dazzlingly white smiles of Saudi Arabians.

college to more productive use than women would. As a result, less money was spent on universities and colleges for women than on facilities for men even though Saudi women consistently achieve higher levels of academic excellence at the secondary level. In the late 1990s the government began moving toward creating more higher education opportunities for women. University and vocational education is also free. In 1998 the country had 7 universities and 66 colleges for men and a single university and 10 colleges for women.

In addition, there were about a dozen teacher-training colleges, 30 educational institutions for handicapped children, and about 30 vocational training institutions. Specialized education in engineering is offered at the University of Petroleum and Minerals at Dhahran on the Persian Gulf coast. The Islamic University at Medina provides religious law studies.

Today, as a result of the government's commitment to improving education, the literacy rate (defined as the percentage of people fifteen and older who can read) is 63 percent. According to government figures, 60 percent finish elementary and middle school and almost 50 percent go on to high school. About half of high school graduates elect to attend college or universities in the kingdom.

Students selected to receive government funding to study abroad receive money for tuition, lodging, board, and transportation. Those intending to study science or technology receive additional funds. A religious rule that prohibits women from traveling without their closest male relative as a chaperon discourages females from studying abroad. Consequently, today almost three times as many Saudi men study outside the country on government scholarships. Male students are paid extra if they marry before leaving Saudi Arabia and take their wives and children with them. The government also offers to pay the school tuition for wives who want to study abroad with their husbands, all part of a plan to help Saudi citizens avoid the moral temptations and cultural confusions that might arise from living alone abroad. Despite reductions in government-subsidized education abroad, there are still about five thousand Saudi students studying in the United States and Europe at any given time.

The government of Saudi Arabia has always intended that public education include religion. One of the primary purposes of the kingdom's education policy is to promote the basic elements of Islam as the correct way to live. At the elementary school level, an average of nine periods a week are devoted to religious subjects, eight periods per week at the middle school level. At the secondary level, less time is spent on religious topics, although students are encouraged to study Islam on their own and most do. Islamic studies have been the traditional topic of Arabian higher education, but religious leaders are concerned about the recent decline in these programs, which are attracting a smaller percentage of students than at any other time in Arabia's history.

CONCLUSION

After decades of intense modernization, Saudi Arabia's cities have become highly developed and technologically sophisticated. Excellent hospitals, clinics, schools, colleges, and universities offer free medical care and education to all Saudi citizens. Shopping malls display Paris fashions, supermarkets sell fresh vegetables flown in from the all over the world, and restaurants offer Mexican, Chinese, or French cuisine. Yet women may not eat in the restaurants with a man who is not a close relative and many services and stores have separate hours for male and female customers. Suburban neighborhoods of single-family homes with swimming pools mingle with retail districts and industrial parks while cellular phone networks, cable television, and satellite communications systems make life in Saudi Arabia surprisingly similar to life in a Western city.

When night falls and the workday ends, Saudi Arabian families like to drive to restaurants, markets, and souks to buy traditional meals or Western-style fast food and shop for Arabic wares or European fashions. Though they live with a mixture of the modern and the traditional, Saudi Arabians retain their sense of family life and Muslim identity.

5

CULTURAL AND POLITICAL VALUES

All cultural and political expression in Saudi Arabia is guided—and restricted—by the kingdom's strict Islam-based laws and by a monarchy determined to maintain absolute control over its citizens. Art, music, literature, and even architecture reflect the strong influence of the styles and forms described in Islam's most holy book, the Quran. Public behavior, political commentary, and news reporting also come under the close scrutiny and tight control of the nation's leaders, who believe political action should arise from the deeply conservative religious principles of Saudi Arabia's Wahhabi Islam.

THE MEDIA AND CENSORSHIP

In Saudi Arabia, strict censorship of the news has been practiced since the kingdom's founding. Special ministers appointed by the royal family oversee all news reporting, television programming, book publishing, and information available over the Internet. Stories critical of the royal family and their domestic or international policies are censored and rarely, if ever, reach the public. Newspapers, magazines, and television stations that try to present any sort of criticism of the nation's leaders can expect to be banned or shut down. Even websites that post unflattering commentary about Saudi Arabia or its leaders have a way of disappearing.

In the early 1990s, for example, the Arabic language daily newspaper, *Al-Hayat*, published an article that criticized the royal family's handling of an extramarital affair involving one of the princesses. The couple at the center of the scandal was executed. The Saudi government responded swiftly by banning sales of the paper throughout the kingdom. According to the paper's editor-in-chief, Jihad Khazen, this brush with angry Saudi officials almost put him out of business. Following this incident, Khazen initiated a strict policy of not allowing anything negative about Saudi Arabian leaders or policies to appear in the paper. Since then *Al-Hayat* has grown to the largest Arabic language newspaper in the world with circulation in sixteen countries.

Political opposition is equally unwelcome in Saudi Arabia. Beginning in 1978 Saudi officials, intent on silencing political opponents, began a drive to gain control of the world's Arabic-language media. The government purchased all kinds of media outlets outright. Those broadcasting and publishing companies they could not buy were often dependent on funding and advertising from Saudi sources, so the Saudis were able to specify rigid standards of news coverage for these companies under threat of withdrawing advertising and funding. Today, either directly or indirectly, the Saudi Arabian government exercises almost total control over the vast Arabic-language media, not only within the kingdom but worldwide.

The Saudi-controlled Arabic media employ the latest technology, hire the most respected journalists and editors, and produce publications and programming of a quality equal to anything seen in the West. But production quality does not mean editorial freedom. According to Abdul Bari Atwan, editor-in-chief of the London-based Arabic daily newspaper *Al-Quds Al-Arabi*, "In Saudi Arabia the media is like a veiled woman. Beneath the veil you may have the finest dressing—the best technology, the best writers and

Strict censorship of newspapers and the Internet influences the information available to Saudis.

THE FIRST MUSLIM ASTRONAUT

Strict Wahhabi Muslims, who generally believe that Islam prohibits any form of technology that did not exist in Muhammad's day (the seventh century), must have been unhappy with Prince Sultan Ibn Salman Ibn Abdul Aziz in 1985. That year Prince Sultan became the first Muslim astronaut, orbiting the earth as payload specialist aboard the U.S. space shuttle *Discovery*. Later that year, U.S. president Ronald Reagan honored Prince Sultan's contribution to the space program in a presentation at the White House.

During his flight on the *Discovery*, Prince Sultan helped launch three communications satellites, including one for the Arab Satellite Communications Organization (Arabsat). He also conducted a series of onboard experiments designed by Saudi scientists, and he personally narrated a guided tour of the spacecraft's interior that was shown live on Saudi television. While in orbit he also held a phone conversation with Saudi King Fahd. Then, in a move reminiscent of Ibn Saud when he brought television to Saudi Arabia, the prince united tradition and technology by reading the Quran on live television.

Prince Sultan, a devout Muslim, reported that performing his prayers while facing Mecca, as all Muslims must do five times each day, presented some interesting problems. There is no record about whether it was more difficult for the prince to kneel down in zero gravity or figure out which way to turn in an orbiting spacecraft in order to face Mecca.

journalists, the finest offices. But it is veiled, completely covered in black. It is censored."[3]

And like a veiled woman, news reporting in Saudi Arabia hides much. Editor Atwan, whose own publication at times has been banned in Saudi Arabia, adds: "The Saudi press doesn't discuss anything about Saudi Arabia. . . . [As a result there is no public information about] how many people are in prison or any statistics on road accidents for fear that such reporting might be construed as a criticism of the king or his government."[4]

Government control also extends beyond the media in Saudi Arabia. The deeply held religious views of the country's leaders control or at least influence every aspect of cultural expression in the kingdom.

MUSIC AND DANCE

Wahhabi Islam forbids public displays of music and dance except in the case of all-male performances of traditional religious or tribal works. In the privacy of their own homes, however, many Saudi citizens enjoy both music and dance. Although radio and television have introduced Western and other styles of music, Western music enjoys little popularity in Saudi Arabia. Saudi tastes lean toward traditional Arabic music, which usually includes a singer backed by various string instruments and drums. Several extremely popular Arabic singers, such as the beloved Lebanese female vocalist Fairouz, enjoy superstar status throughout Saudi Arabia as well as other Arabic-speaking countries.

Traditional folk music and dance also have a large following in Saudi Arabia. One organization, the Saudi Arabian Society for Culture and the Arts, began an ambitious project in the early 1980s to preserve a record of traditional Arabian folk music and dances. This organization has catalogued more than fifty still-active folk dance and music groups, many of which perform the national dance of Saudi Arabia—a sword dance from the Najd region known as the ardha. The ardha is an ancient folk tradition that combines singers and dancers with a singing narrator. The all-male ensemble, dressed in colorful costumes and brandishing swords, dance shoulder to shoulder while the singers and drummers perform a traditional musical accompaniment and the narrator sings the words to famous poems about bravery, loyalty, and God.

AN ARABIAN ODE TO "CRAZY LOVE"

In Saudi Arabia and other Arabic-speaking countries, the lyrics of many popular songs feature modernized versions of romantic poems that were written before the time of Muhammad, more than a thousand years ago. The authors of these ancient poems include Umar, called the "prince of Arabian erotic poetry" by the historian Philip Hitti, and Jamil, a romantic poet who lived in the Hijaz during the eighth century and wrote about his love for his sweetheart Buthaynah. The most popular ancient lyrical poet, however, was and continues to be a man from Najd named Qays, known more commonly by his nickname, Majnun Layla.

As the story goes, Qays fell madly in love with a woman from his own tribe named Layla, and Layla fell in love with Qays in return, but she was forced by her father to marry another man. Brokenhearted, Qays spent the rest of his life wandering crazed and half-naked through his native land singing songs about the beauty of his beloved Layla. Eventually he became known as Majnun Layla (literally, "Crazy for Layla"). Centuries later, Majnun Layla and his lost love continue to provide the subject material for countless songs dedicated to the power of undying love.

LITERATURE

Bravery, loyalty, and faith in God, along with the teachings of the Quran, are the dominant themes in the published works of contemporary Saudi writers. The most popular of these works spin tales from famous battles, raids, hunting adventures, or encounters with nature. The stories are enhanced by the lyrical constructions of the Arabic language, whose flowery phrasing treats even the simplest event or sentiment poetically.

Ancient works written before the rise of Islam focus on themes of love, romance, and courage, themes mostly absent from modern Saudi writing. Many of the poems and stories from those early times still survive, due largely to the Arabian love for poetry. Because Muhammad disapproved of romantic poetry, however, few such works were written after the adoption of Islam. Many Saudis consider their most important writer to be Uthman ibn Bishr, who wrote histories of the early days of the Saud clan and other tribes of the Arabian Peninsula.

THE VISUAL ARTS

Islam's influence can also be seen in the visual arts. Calligraphy, the highly decorative writing style practiced as an art form in Saudi Arabia, dates from the seventh century, the first century of Islam. The primary subject matter of Arabic calligraphy has always been the Quran, and it is the most respected form of Islamic art in Saudi Arabia. Several Saudi museums collect and display rare works of calligraphy, and calligraphy schools and competitions keep the art alive by encouraging new generations of skilled calligraphers. Today, calligraphy produced in Saudi Arabia is seen on metalwork, ceramics, glass, textiles, and architecture. Ornate calligraphic inscriptions can be found as adornments on the interior walls of mosques and many public and private office buildings and homes.

A thirteenth-century Quran page written in ornate calligraphy.

THE SAUDI MASTER OF MINIATURE CONSTRUCTION

When Darwish Ali Salamah retired from the Saudi Arabian air force, he finally had time to express his artistic longings. He decided to build his own kingdom, a fantastically detailed, miniature kingdom with perfect replicas of buildings and other structures from all over Saudi Arabia.

As an air force pilot, Ali Salamah flew to all regions of the country and used that opportunity to study the various architectural styles found in the kingdom. This way, he already had a wealth of firsthand knowledge of the kingdom's rich architectural heritage by the time he started building his miniature kingdom. Today in the garden of his home in Saudi Arabia, he reigns over a small kingdom filled with miniature replicas of buildings and natural structures from all over the country. There are mosques, villas, forts, caravanscrais, mountains, wadis, and dunes of Saudi Arabian red sand, all built with accuracy and fantastic attention to detail.

In constructing these miniatures, many less than six inches tall, Ali Salamah also reproduced the building methods of full-size structures. He used iron bars and wire to reinforce the concrete that makes up the walls and roofs, rendering them so sturdy that almost every building can support the weight of an adult standing on its roof. Some of the miniature structures also serve as planters, and trees and shrubbery sprout from them.

Ali Salamah's skills are not limited to only Saudi Arabian styles. For example, he once received a request from an American to build a miniature version of the man's home in Philadelphia. Based on some photographs and verbal descriptions, the retired pilot built a perfect replica of the American's home right down to the street address.

The visual arts in Saudi Arabia are also expressed in the country's architecture, which, like other forms of expression in Saudi Arabia, bears the firm imprint of Islam. The most important architectural form throughout Saudi Arabia's history has been the mosque, the Islamic house of worship. The mosque is the central feature in any village, town, or city, and government buildings, houses, and souks are laid out around the mosque.

Mosques are easily distinguished from all other buildings by their eye-catching domes, pillars, arches, and the slender towers known as minarets. The typical minaret has one or more balconies from which calls to prayer are issued. Intricate mosaics of geometric, floral, and abstract patterns adorn the walls, ceilings, and floors of most mosques, and the domes are frequently blue or gold.

Even among the modern high-rise buildings in Saudi Arabia's bustling cities, the large, decorative mosques stand out.

The mosque, the Islamic house of worship, has been the most important architectural form throughout Saudi Arabia's history.

But now they are surrounded by a profusion of new styles. During the second half of the twentieth century Saudi Arabia's urban centers started developing along the lines of American-style cities with residential suburbs, shopping centers, and industrial parks. Ultramodern structures that would look right at home in Los Angeles or Dallas are now common in Jiddah, Riyadh, and other large cities in the kingdom.

The new styles of buildings contrast sharply with Saudi Arabia's traditional architecture and design principles. The country's outspoken conservatives, objecting to the growth of Western-style business, government, and residential buildings, view these changes as threats to Saudi society and values.

SPORTS

One of the few aspects of Saudi culture not directly influenced by religion is sport. Forty-three percent of the population is younger than fifteen, so it is no surprise that a large part of the population participates in sports. Soccer is by far the most popular sport in the country. Whether in stadiums or empty lots, adults and children play soccer all year long, even during the hottest part of the summer. This passion is reflected in the considerable success of the Saudi national soccer team in international competition.

Volleyball, basketball, tennis, squash, and archery are other popular sports in the kingdom, and the popularity of golf is booming. Along the coasts, Saudis and foreigners alike enjoy boating, fishing, and scuba diving.

During cooler weather, many Saudi men go out into the desert to practice the traditional Bedouin sport of hunting with falcons. Falconry, an ancient sport, has enjoyed a resurgence of interest since hunting with guns was banned in an

TRADITIONAL HOSPITALITY AND TRADITIONAL DOORS

Hospitality is the very essence of Arabian culture. In traditional Arabian homes, hospitality begins at the front door. Doors are important in Saudi Arabia; in their design, construction, and decoration they reflect uniquely Arab and Islamic architectural values.

Though traditional Saudi homes are constructed from a variety of materials, including coral along the Red Sea and Persian Gulf, stone in the highlands and northern Najd, and mud in the desert and oases, wood has very seldom been used. Simply too scarce in Arabia to use as a construction material, this precious commodity is reserved mostly for decorative purposes, in particular, doors.

In many parts of the kingdom, entrances are decorated with wooden frames that have been ornately decorated with Arabic calligraphy welcoming visitors and blessing the inhabitants of the home. In some regions, especially Najd, wooden doors were intricately carved, and in some areas they are painted in bright colors.

Decorations and carvings in classic Islamic geometric designs adorn not only old and traditional but also modern doors. Present-day architects and city planners, recognizing the cultural and historical value of old doors, have begun incorporating these uniquely Arabian styles into modern residential and commercial projects. Reflecting a renewed appreciation of the country's ancient roots, the Saudi government encourages the preservation of old doors and other remaining elements of traditional architecture, an appreciation that was lacking during much of the modernization of the country that followed the discovery of oil.

Traditional Arabian doors are often decorated with classic Islamic geometric designs.

Soccer players from Saudi Arabia (left) and Spain fight for the ball during an international championship match.

effort to conserve the few species of larger animals that still live on the Arabian Peninsula. The sport involves capturing and training wild falcons to hunt other birds and small mammals. Many Saudi falconers own specialized all-wheel-drive convertibles with built-in perches for their falcons. It is not unusual to see such vehicles, with several blindfolded falcons holding tightly onto their perches, bounding across the desert in search of game.

Another traditional sport, racing horses and camels, is also very popular. Each year the King's Cup Camel Race is held in the desert near Riyadh, and more than two thousand camels and riders take part. The spectacle of thousands of camels, their riders bouncing atop them, racing across a long straight track in the middle of the desert reminds the Saudis of their nomadic heritage. Straight-track horse sprints are also popular and members of the royal family can often be seen in attendance at camel and horse races. Many wealthy Saudis breed camels and Arabian horses.

Though sporting events are not religious in nature, Saudi Arabia's religious foundation appears even here because behavior at sporting events, like all other public venues, is governed by religious law.

THE RELIGIOUS POLICE

Because of the influence of Wahhabi Islam, public behavior in Saudi Arabia is extremely conservative. In addition to having a regular police force, Saudi Arabia has an internal security force whose sole duty is the enforcement of religious law. These independent and highly visible religious police are called the mutawwan. About twenty thousand mutawwan receive government salaries, but countless other Islamic watchdogs who are simply self-appointed religious vigilantes also patrol public areas.

The mutawwan zealously enforce the laws of Islam. Usually accompanied by regular uniformed police, they accost or even arrest foreigners for improper dress or other infractions of Islamic law, including drinking alcohol or the association of a female with a male to whom she is not related. In many areas of Saudi Arabia, particularly in Riyadh and other towns in the central part of the kingdom, the mutawwan pressure all women to wear the full-length abaya in public.

Mutawwan have the authority to ask for proof that a man and woman appearing together in public, whether they are Arab or foreign, are married or related. A woman arrested for socializing with a man who is not her relative may be

---

GOLFING IN SAUDI ARABIA

In spite of its arid climate and jokes that the entire country is one big sand trap, Saudi Arabia is home to a number of golf courses. Golf-playing employees of American oil companies built the first golf courses in the kingdom near Dhahran in the late 1940s. Until recently, however, the only courses that existed were entirely sand and gravel with "greens" that were actually "browns" of oiled sand.

Today, despite the scarcity of water, avid golfers have managed to build a number of successful courses that feature not only true grass greens but also fairways green with grass and trees. Most green courses still lack actual bodies of water; instead, sand depressions marked with blue stakes indicate that they are "water hazards." Riyadh was home to the first entirely grass course in Saudi Arabia, and now there are half a dozen grassy courses as well as a dozen more of the older-style desert courses.

More than half of the existing courses opened during the 1990s, in response to the increasing in popularity of golf in the kingdom. One of the busiest of the new grass courses in Riyadh is named the Arizona Golf Resort. It looks like it was imported from Phoenix or Tucson, complete with an upscale southwestern adobe residential development that includes a baseball field, equestrian center, inline skating park, roller hockey court, and four-lane bowling alley.

charged with prostitution. Some restaurants, particularly fast-food outlets, refuse to serve a woman who is not accompanied by a close male relative, including a woman who wants to eat by herself. Though these restrictions are not always posted, sometimes the mutawwan will arrest women who violate this policy. Nor are women allowed to drive motor vehicles or ride bicycles on public roads in Saudi Arabia. In addition, public dancing, music, and movies are forbidden throughout the kingdom except in fenced compounds where foreigners live.

The mutawwan have earned a reputation for fanaticism and brutality, known to hit people with sticks for the slightest infraction of the public morality laws. Public flogging with a cane or switch is the usual punishment for offenses against religion and morality, such as public drunkenness, gambling, and neglecting prayer or fasting requirements. The mutawwan usually carry out the flogging themselves, painfully but without breaking the skin. The intention of public flogging is to degrade rather than cripple the offender and serve as a deterrent to others. Though the royal family has frequently

Some restaurants in Saudi Arabia refuse to serve women who are not accompanied by a close male relative.

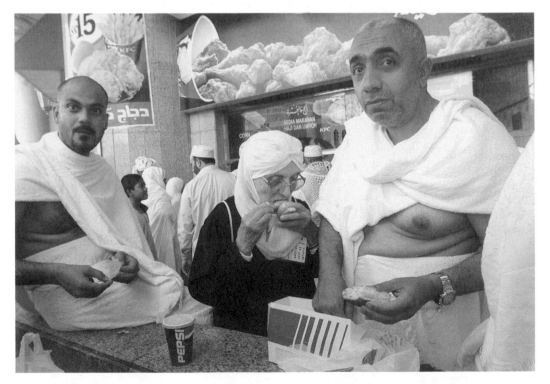

disagreed with the methods of the mutawwan, the government has been reluctant to take up the issue with the ulama whose approval is required before the majority of the population will accept a political or social change.

CRIME AND PUNISHMENT

Under Saudi Arabian law, serious crimes merit serious consequences. Repeated theft is punishable by amputation of the right hand, administered under anesthetic. Because most meals in Saudi Arabia are eaten by hand from a communal bowl and only the right hand may touch the food, this punishment effectively bans the convicted thief from society. The severity of this punishment has led to a slight softening of the law in recent years; now if the thief repents and makes restitution before the case is brought before a judge, the punishment can be reduced. Furthermore, the victim of the crime may demand repayment rather than amputation of the thief's right hand, and in some cases the victim is even permitted to pardon the criminal. In a typical year perhaps ten hand amputations are carried out for repeated thievery in Saudi Arabia.

Crimes punishable by the death sentence in Saudi Arabia include murder, serious attacks on the Islam religion, adultery, sabotage, and, since 1987, drug smuggling. Under certain conditions, rape and armed robbery are also punishable by execution. Although most executions are carried out by beheading, some are by firing squad or stoning.

In 1987, based on a new ruling by the ulama, drug smugglers and those who receive or distribute drugs from abroad became subject to the death sentence. First-time offenders face some combination of prison terms, floggings, and fines; those convicted a second time face execution. Within two years, this ruling, coupled with a new antidrug campaign, resulted in a 60 percent drop in drug addiction and 26 percent reduction in drug use. Saudi officials now claim that the kingdom has the lowest rate of drug addiction in the world, which they attribute to harsh punishment and the religious convictions of ordinary Saudis. Nevertheless, drug use has persisted among wealthy young Saudis who acquire the habit abroad, and even several members of the royal family have been caught in posession of drugs.

The incidence of crime in Saudi Arabia remains low compared with crime rates in other modern countries. Violent street crime is particularly rare. Government officials and ordinary citizens alike attribute the high level of public safety in the kingdom to the severity of the punishment for crime and the rigid system of enforcement. Supporters of severe penalties believe that punishments mandated by Islamic law, such as public beheading or stoning, remind potential murderers and thieves that severe penalties await anyone who breaks the law.

According to the Saudi Arabian Ministry of Finance and National Economy, the most common crimes are theft, violations involving alcohol (production, sale, and/or consumption), public fights and quarreling, and offenses against morality. There is very little murder, arson, forgery, or fraud in the kingdom.

CONCLUSION

As in so many other aspects of Saudi Arabian life, cultural and political values are determined largely by religious values: conservative dress, conservative literature, and conservative behavior. Freedom of political expression is not allowed, and diversions like going to the movies or dancing, activities taken for granted by most Westerners, are almost nonexistent in Saudi Arabia. Besides ever-present forms of religious self-expression, the character of the Saudi Arabian finds expression in family life and hospitality, and in activities like falconry and playing soccer. As it has been for centuries, the cultural and political life of Saudi Arabia continues to be expressed in terms of Islamic principles.

FACING THE
CHALLENGES AHEAD

Saudi Arabia is the largest of all the Arab countries and one of the richest nations on earth. Its immense wealth has given Saudi Arabia a great deal of influence in world and regional affairs. Its size and deeply held religious and political views, as well as its role as guardian of sacred religious sites, has added weight to the kingdom's position as a key player in the troubled Middle East.

However, interaction with so many peoples and nations beyond its own borders has come at a price for Saudi Arabia. Isolated no longer, the kingdom must now contend with a flood of mostly unwelcome outside influences on its people and way of life. It has also been forced to acknowledge its limitations and even to rethink traditional alliances. The Persian Gulf War of 1990 underscored Saudi Arabia's vulnerabilities like no other event in recent history and forced the country's leaders to consider alternate routes to the future.

THE PERSIAN GULF WAR AND ITS AFTERMATH

In 1990 Saddam Hussein, the dictator of Iraq, Saudi Arabia's neighbor to the north, marched his armies into Kuwait and seized that small oil-rich country. In the face of this aggression from a former ally, Saudi Arabia was forced to change its foreign policy in a way that alienated other Muslim countries and provoked criticism of the kingdom's ability to protect Islam's most holy shrines. Saudi Arabia's leaders, fearing a full-scale invasion and recognizing its military inability to resist the Iraqis, turned to the United States for military help. This deeply offended Muslims around the world who saw that Saudi Arabia was about to become the temporary base for almost half a million non-Muslim soldiers who would soon be attacking and killing fellow Muslims if Saddam Hussein did not pull his army out of Kuwait.

American forces mobilized in Saudi Arabia in 1990 in response to Saddam Hussein's invasion of Kuwait.

Iraq did not back down in the face of the massed forces consisting mostly of American and Saudi Arabian soldiers. In January 1991 a brief war to liberate Kuwait ensued. Many of the planes that bombed Iraqi targets took off from airfields in Saudi Arabia; Iraq retaliated by firing Scud missiles at Saudi cities and invading the Saudi town of Khafji, near the Kuwait border. Iraqi forces briefly held Khafji until the Saudi army pushed them back. During the next few days Allied forces moved into Kuwait and quickly drove out the Iraqi forces to end the war.

The Persian Gulf War cost Saudi Arabia $48 billion, almost half of the country's annual income from oil. This catastrophic expense forced the Saudis to borrow money for the first time in twenty years, but the financial cost was only part of what the kingdom had to pay for the war. Before the Iraqi forces fled Kuwait, they set fire to refineries and blew up oil wells, pipelines, and tankers. This sabotage sent massive quantities of oil pouring into the Persian Gulf, creating the world's largest oil spill, estimated to be about 8 million barrels. Currents carried the oil south, where it fouled almost the entire eastern shoreline of Saudi Arabia, including vast areas that had been the feeding and breeding grounds for birds, fish, and shrimp. Oil fires continued to burn for months in the Kuwait desert, and dense clouds of smoke drifted south, where airborne particles triggered asthma and bronchitis attacks throughout the eastern provinces of Saudi Arabia.

Shocked by the economic and environmental costs of the war and stung by a strong backlash against further military assistance from the United States, Saudi Arabia's leaders began a fundamental shift in the kingdom's foreign policy. After the war the country began builiding a stronger military, which announced to its neighbors that Saudi Arabia intended to take a more forceful role in maintaining stability in the region. At the same time Saudi Arabia cut back on financial aid to other Arab countries. Giving less money to its Arab allies, building a stronger military, and refusing to abandon its close ties with the United States, Saudi Arabia risked the disapproval of the other Arab nations as it moved toward a position of greater power in the Middle East.

CHANGING ALLIANCES

Another effect of the Persian Gulf War was the blurring of the traditional lines distinguishing political friends from enemies. Iraq, long thought to be a friend to Saudi Arabia, showed itself to be otherwise. Iran, with whom Saudi Arabia had experienced strained relations for years, showed itself to be more friend than enemy during the war. Iran (a long-time enemy of Iraq) came down squarely on the side of those nations opposing Saddam Hussein's incursions into Kuwait and Saudi Arabia.

Iran's support of Saudi Arabia and Kuwait during the Persian Gulf War marked the beginning of an era of improved relations after two decades of discord between the two countries. The trouble began after the Iranian revolution against the pro-West shah in 1970, which resulted in a fundamentalist government at the head of the new Islamic Republic of Iran. At first Saudi Arabia welcomed the new regime because of its adherence to Islamic principles. Iranians, however, considered Saudi Arabia too friendly with the United States and the Iranian press was filled with anti-Saudi Arabian sentiments. Then in 1987 Iranian pilgrims held a huge demonstration in Mecca to express their opposition to Saudi Arabia's ties with the United States. The demonstration turned violent and over four hundred people were killed in the ensuing riot. Reacting to the deaths of these Iranians in Mecca, an angry mob attacked the Saudi Arabian embassy in Iran's capital and beat several Saudi officials so badly that one died. Consequently Saudi Arabia broke diplomatic relations with Iran, which made it impossible for Iranians to obtain the visas they needed to make the pilgramage to Mecca.

Iran and Saudi Arabia finally put aside their differences and began talks after the Persian Gulf War. Toward the end of 1991 the two countries restored diplomatic relations and Iranian pilgrims could once again go to Mecca. Following the war, Iran and Saudi Arabia embarked on a path of cooperation in maintaining regional security.

HELP FOR THE PALESTINIANS

Regional issues have long occupied Saudi Arabia in another context. Saudi leaders have devoted a great deal of time and money to the quest of Palestinian Arabs for an independant state, a quest that has great support among Saudi citizens. For decades Saudi Arabia served as the primary financial backer of the Palestinian Liberation Organization (PLO), which represents the Palestinian people. Hardly a day goes by that Saudi Arabian newspapers do not feature a front-page story about the Palestinians. The Saudi Arabian government blames ongoing political instability and conflict in the Middle East on the failure to create a Palestinian state. Saudi Arabians consider the Palestinian problem their problem too, not just because of the kingdom's huge financial in-

 WAR OVER A RED SEA ISLAND

In 1998, troops from Yemen, a Muslim country located at the southwestern corner of the Arabian Peninsula, took over Duwaima Island in the Red Sea, an island claimed by both Saudi Arabia and Yemen. The Yemenis fired on Saudi border guards; since that first clash, each side has accused the other of starting numerous skirmishes that have resulted in several dozen casualties on both sides.

This conflict may have deeper implications than simply deciding which country owns Duwaima Island. The monarchy of Saudi Arabia became uneasy when two smaller countries united to form the democratic new Yemen, making it the only nation on the entire Arabian Peninsula to have a democratic style of government. Some reports indicate that Saudi Arabia might attempt to sabotage this democratic regime with military bullying and by helping Yemenis opposed to the current government to undermine it.

vestment, but also because they believe all Arabs have a moral obligation to help the Palestinians find a home. Saudi Arabia has pledged to continue its support—both financial and political—for the Palestinian cause.

SAUDI ARABIA'S RELATIONSHIP WITH THE UNITED STATES

Regional issues such as the ongoing conflict between the Palestinians and the Israelis on many occasions have strained relations between Saudi Arabia and another of its longtime allies: the United States. Saudi Arabia and the United States have enjoyed a close relationship for more than half a century, beginning with the instrumental role played by American companies in developing the oil fields of eastern Arabia. Since then the United States has supplied vast amounts of military equipment and technological aid and become a major trading partner. Over the years many U.S.-educated Saudi Arabians have returned home with a deepened appreciation of American values. Nevertheless

Though Saudi Arabia has long supported the desire of the Palestinian people for an independent state, Palestinian refugees like these are still without a homeland.

anti-American sentiment in Saudi Arabia is growing, chiefly because of U.S. support for Israel and the increased American military presence in the kingdom. As a result Saudi Arabia's relationship with the United States has become one of the major challenges facing the kingdom.

The friendly and cooperative relationship between the governments of the United States and Saudi Arabia that dates from World War II has frequently been strained over the issue of American support for Israel. Like the rest of the Arab world, Saudi Arabia opposed the 1948 establishment of Israel in the former mostly Arab territory of Palestine, and for many years the Saudis refused to acknowledge the right of Israel to exist. While Saudi Arabia has since softened its position, it suspects Israel of trying to sabotage the kingdom's traditionally strong ties with the United States. During the 1970s and 1980s, Saudi suspicions seemed to be confirmed when American politicians regularly opposed arms sales to Saudi Arabia on the grounds that the Saudis might use them against Israel. Despite assurances from Saudi officials that the weapons were necessary for their country's defense, the American Congress often reduced or canceled proposed arms sales to Saudi Arabia. From the Saudi perspective, the United States seemed to be backing out of its formal commitment to support Saudi Arabian defenses.

Any uncertainties the Saudi Arabians may have felt were quelled by the American response to Iraq's invasion of Kuwait. After the Persian Gulf War, however, Saudi Arabia again encountered resistance to arms sales in Congress, although Saudi cooperation in the war against Iraq had clearly demonstrated that the kingdom needed military equipment for its own defense. The positive feelings between the two countries created during the war have eroded somewhat and Saudi perceptions that Americans treat them as a less valuable ally have prompted resentment. With anti-American sentiment growing, the safety of American military and civilian personnel stationed in the kingdom is questionable.

During the 1990s, two terrorist bombings struck Saudi installations where large numbers of U.S. military personnel were housed. Dozens of Americans were killed and hundreds more injured. The U.S. government believed both bombings were financed by Osama bin Ladin, a Saudi expatriate businessman with ties to radical Islamic fundamentalist move-

THE FUTURE OF AMERICAN AND SAUDI RELATIONS: FROM MILITARY AID TO BUSINESS PARTNERS

Many Americans and Saudis hope to see Saudi Arabia's foreign policy shift from its 1990s preoccupation with regional security issues back to doing business together. There are many signs that this is exactly what Saudi Arabia's leaders want. By 1999, more than thirty-five thousand Americans were living and working in Saudi Arabia. During that year over two hundred joint ventures between the two countries produced tens of billions of dollars in sales to Saudi Arabia of American aircraft, telecommunications, and power projects. In 1999 American investments in the kingdom exceeded $5 billion, which equaled almost half of all the foreign investment in Saudi Arabia.

In 1996, Prince Bandar bin Sultan bin Abdul Aziz, Saudi Arabia's ambassador to the United States, said in a book titled *A Business Guide to the Kingdom of Saudi Arabia* and published by the Royal Embassy of Saudi Arabia in Washington, D.C., "The relationship between the Kingdom of Saudi Arabia and the United States of America was primarily economic in character at the time of the late 1930s when American companies discovered vast oil reserves in the Kingdom. . . . In the past decade Saudi-U.S. relations have shifted in priorities to the security and welfare of the Kingdom. . . . This unique relationship has provided the right atmosphere for a healthy U.S.-Saudi business partnership to develop. . . . Commercial interests survive longer than strategic interests. When countries do business together, they stay together."

Prince Bandar's words sound almost like he was describing a marriage, and some Americans think a business marriage between the two countries would benefit both and contribute to peace in the world at the same time. Echoing Prince Bandar's words, in 1996 Secretary of Commerce Mickey Kantor stated (also in *A Business Guide to the Kingdom of Saudi Arabia*), "Saudi Arabia is our close ally and our most important trading partner in the Middle East and North Africa region. This relationship is based on mutual strategic interests and the very real benefits of our long-term commercial and economic partnership. Strategic considerations have made us allies, but the ties of trade have brought us truly together."

ments. Saudi Arabian investigators, however, placed the blame on terrorist groups with roots in Iran or Syria. Whoever was responsible, these bombings represented a deadly escalation in the efforts of ultraconservative groups within Saudi Arabia to drive all non-Muslims from the country.

REVIVAL OF ULTRACONSERVATIVE ISLAM

Since the 1980s, many parts of the Muslim world have experienced a sharp rise in ultraconservative, Islamic political movements. Labeled fundamentalist Muslims by the Western press, these ultraconservative Islamic groups are seeking to turn the countries where they live into Muslim states governed by strict

Islamic laws and conservative social ideals. Saudi Arabia, whose only constitution is the Quran, has always claimed to be exactly this sort of Islamic state, but to the ultraconservatives the policies of the Saudi government are still too liberal.

Though they are a minority in the kingdom, the ultraconservatives wield considerable influence. They have managed to shift Saudi society in a conservative direction, away from Western ideals of social equality. This rise of ultraconservative Islam, both inside and outside Saudi Arabia, is challenging the kingdom to redefine the nature of its religion-based society.

POLITICS AND THE MONARCHY

Since its founding in 1932 the absolute monarchy of Saudi Arabia has been a force for conservative politics that has never provided any opportunity for representative government—no elections, no political parties, no freedom of speech. In quiet yet persistent opposition to both the monarchy and the ultraconservatives, Saudi liberals have pressed the king to create a democratic parliament, reduce the power of religion in society, and create an independent judicial sys-

American and Saudi investigators examine the damage caused by a 1996 terrorist bombing of a Saudi Arabian installation that housed U.S. troops.

tem similar to that of the United States. In what many hoped would be a meaningful step toward a more democratic Saudi Arabia, the king actually did create a parliament in 1992. It turned out, however, to be dominated by the ulama, making it simply another force for preserving conservative policies. As proof, in recent years the regime has moved toward even stricter application of Islamic laws within the country, partially in response to critics of the government's military cooperation with non-Muslim countries. As a result, today Saudi Arabian society and politics are even more conservative than in past decades.

The ruling royal family, led by King Fahd, will very likely guide Saudi Arabia's future.

There is little doubt that the royal family intends the political control of Saudi Arabia to remain in the hands of the king and his advisers. With the cry for reform becoming as loud as the cry for more conservative policies, Saudi Arabia may face serious confrontations. However, if the Saudi government's response to the growing women's movement in the kingdom is any indication, confrontation will bring little in the way of change.

THE ISSUE OF WOMEN IN SAUDI ARABIA

The plight of women in Saudi society was highlighted in 1990 when about fifty women from upper-class families staged a protest in the country's capital to obtain automobile driving rights for female adults. Though there is no formal law barring women from driving, it is universally understood that women are not allowed to drive in Saudi Arabia. So when these women dismissed their drivers and started driving their own cars, it caused a national crisis. Several of the women were fired from their jobs and the local newspapers treated them as if they had committed a terrible crime. Even the king made an announcement harshly criticizing the protestors. According to an article by Eleanor Abdella Doumato written soon after the incident, "A leading Wahhabi deliberative body issued a fatwa [authoritative religious opinion] that found that 'women should not be allowed to drive motor vehicles as the sharia [religious law] instructs that things that degrade or harm the dignity of women must be prevented.'"[4]

The Islamic world takes a considerably different view of women than Western countries do. Islam considers the family to be the basic social unit, a belief with which many Westerners agree, but strict Muslims believe that women must remain at home and care for the family or else the family unit will disintegrate. Thus women in Saudi Arabia are denied many things that Western women take for granted, like driving, wearing whatever clothing they desire in public, and mingling socially with men who are not close relatives. Furthermore, Saudi women have fewer career opportunities and are held to higher standards of moral conduct compared with men.

From their viewpoint, most Saudi Arabians see the liberalization of Western women as the major reason behind the violence and other social problems of countries like the United States, so the prospect of changing the role of Saudi women in the near future seems dim. Dissatisfaction with the current state of affairs, however, is likely to grow as more Saudis gain access to the outer world through sources like the Internet, making the place of women in society a continuing challenge for the kingdom.

CONCLUSION

Considering the nature of its society, the arrival of its spectacular wealth, and the explosive growth of recent decades, Saudi Arabia has remained remarkably stable. This young nation, however, is now facing an unprecedented set of challenges.

Along with regional security issues, shifting alliances, and grave financial setbacks, today Saudi Arabia also faces growing internal turmoil. Increasing resistance to the absolute powers of the monarchy, rising demands for greater rights for women, and escalations in the continuing conflict between modernization and Islamic fundamentalism have lead to more repressive measures from the monarchy. Saudi Arabians are relying on their religious foundation and oil wealth to meet these difficult challenges and in the process define their country's position in the modern world.

FACTS ABOUT
SAUDI ARABIA

GEOGRAPHY

Location: Middle East, bordering the Persian Gulf and the Red Sea, north of Yemen

Area:
Total land area: 764,627 sq. mi., slightly more than one-fifth the size of the United States

Land boundaries:
Total: 2,737 mi.
border countries: Iraq, 505 miles; Jordan, 451 miles; Kuwait, 138 miles; Oman, 419 miles; Qatar, 37 miles; UAE, 283 miles; Yemen, 904 mi.

Coastline: 1,637 mi.

Climate: Harsh, dry desert with great extremes of temperature

Terrain: Mostly uninhabited, sandy desert

Elevation extremes:
Lowest point: Persian Gulf, sea level
Highest point: Jabal Sawda, 10,338 ft.

Natural resources: Petroleum, natural gas, iron ore, gold, copper

Land use:
Arable land: 2%
Permanent crops: 0%
Permanent pastures: 56%
Forests and woodland: 1%
Other: 41% (1993 est.)

Irrigated land: 1,700 sq. mi. (1993 est.)

Natural hazards: Frequent sand and dust storms

POPULATION

Population: 21,504,613 (July 1999 est.), includes 5,321,938 non-nationals (July 1999 est.)

Demographics:
0–14 years: 43% (male 4,705,724; female 4,543,918)
15–64 years: 54% (male 6,925,020; female 4,783,570)
65 years and over: 3% (male 291,449; female 254,932) (1999 est.)

Population growth rate: 3.39% (1999 est.)

Birth rate: 37.38 births/1,000 population (1999 est.)

Death rate: 4.86 deaths/1,000 population (1999 est.)

Net migration rate: 1.4 migrant(s)/1,000 population (1999 est.)

Sex ratio:
Total population: 1.24 male(s)/female (1999 est.)

Infant mortality rate: 38.8 deaths/1,000 live births (1999 est.)

Life expectancy at birth:
Total population: 70.55 years
Male: 68.67 years
Female: 72.53 years (1999 est.)

Ethnic groups: Arab 90%, Afro-Asian 10%

Religions: Muslim 100%

Languages: Arabic

Literacy:
Total population: 62.8%
Male: 71.5%
Female: 50.2% (1995 est.)

GOVERNMENT

Country name: Kingdom of Saudi Arabia ; in Arabic, Al Mamlakah al
Arabiyah as Suudiyah

Type of Government: Monarchy

Capital: Riyadh

Administrative divisions: 13 provinces: Al Bahah, Al Hudud ash
Shamaliyah, Al Jawf, Al Madinah, Al Qasim, Ar Riyad, Ash Shar-
qiyah (Eastern Province), Asir, Ha'il, Jizan, Makkah, Najran, and
Tabuk

Independence: September 23, 1932 (unification)

National holiday: Unification of the Kingdom, September 23 (1932)

Constitution: Based on the Quran and governed according to Sharia
(Islamic law); the Basic Law that describes the government's rights
and responsibilities was introduced in 1993.

Legal system: Based on Islamic law

Voting (Suffrage): None

Executive branch:
Head of government: King and Prime Minister Fahd bin Abd al-
Aziz Al Saud (since June 13, 1982); Crown Prince and First
Deputy Prime Minister Abdallah bin Abd al-Aziz Al Saud
(half-brother to the monarch, heir to the throne since June
13, 1982, acting king from January 1 to February 22, 1996)

Cabinet: Council of Ministers is appointed by the monarch and
includes many royal family members

Elections: None; the monarch is hereditary

Legislative branch: A consultative council (90 members and a chair-
man appointed by the king for four-year terms)

Judicial branch: Supreme Council of Justice

Political parties and leaders: None allowed

Flag description: Green with large white Arabic script (translated as

"There is no God but God; Muhammad Is the Messenger of God")
above a white horizontal saber (the tip points to the hoist side);
green is the traditional color of Islam

ECONOMY

Overview: A well-to-do oil-based economy with strong government
controls over major economic activities, Saudi Arabia has the
largest reserves of petroleum in the world (26% of the proved total), and ranks as the largest exporter of petroleum. The petroleum
sector accounts for roughly 75% of revenues, 40% of GDP, and 90%
of export earnings. About 35% of GDP comes from the private sector. Roughly 4 million foreign workers play an important role in
the Saudi economy, especially in the oil and service sectors. The
Saudi economy was severely hit by the large decline in world oil
prices in 1998. GDP fell by nearly 11%; the budget deficit rose to
$12.3 billion; and the current account recorded a $13 billion
deficit —the first in three years. The government announced plans
to implement large spending cuts in 1999 because of weak oil
prices and will continue to call on greater private-sector involve-
ment in the economy. Shortages of water and rapid population
growth will constrain government efforts to increase self-suffi-
ciency in agricultural products.

Gross Domestic Product (GDP) (by sector):
Agriculture: 6%
Industry: 53%
Services: 41% (1996)

Inflation rate (consumer prices): -0.2% (1998 est.)

Labor force: 7 million
Note: 35% of the population in the 15–64 age group is non-national
(July 1998 est.)

Labor force—by occupation: government 40%; industry, construction,
and oil 25%; services 30%; agriculture 5%

Industries: Crude oil production, petroleum refining, basic petro-
chemicals, cement, two small otool-rolling mills, construction,
fertilizer, plastics

Industrial production growth rate: 1% (1997 est.)

Electricity—production: 95 billion kWh (1996), all from fossil fuel
—consumption: 95 billion kWh (1996)

Agriculture—products: Wheat, barley, tomatoes, melons, dates, citrus,
mutton, chickens, eggs, milk

Total Exports: $59.7 billion (1997); petroleum and petroleum products
90%

Exports by Trade Partner: Japan 18%; U.S. 15%; South Korea 11%; Sin-
gapore 8%; India 4% (1997 est.)

Imports: $26.2 billion (1997) Machinery and equipment, foodstuffs,
chemicals, motor vehicles, textiles

Imports by Trade Partner: U.S. 23%; UK 17%; Japan 8%; Germany 8%;
Italy 5% (1997 est.)

Economic aid: Pledged $100 million in 1993 to fund reconstruction of

Lebanon; since 1993, Saudi Arabia has committed $208 million for assistance to the Palestinians

Currency: 1 Saudi riyal (SR) = 100 halalah

Exchange rate: Saudi riyals (SR) per US$1: 3.7450 (fixed rate since June 1986)

COMMUNICATIONS

Telephones: 1.46 million (1993)

Radio broadcast stations: 43 AM, 13 FM

Television broadcast stations: 117 (1997)

TRANSPORTATION

Railways:
Total: 863 miles

Highways:
total: 100,442 miles
paved: 42,890 miles
unpaved: 57,552 miles (1996 est.)

Pipelines: Crude oil 4,000 miles; petroleum products 93 miles; natural gas 1,364 miles

Ports and harbors: Ad Dammam, Al Jubayl, Duba, Jiddah, Jizan, Rabigh, Ra's al Khafji, Mishab, Ras Tanura, Yanbu' al Bahr, Madinat Yanbu' al Sinaiyah

Airports: 205 (1998 est.)

MILITARY

Military branches: Land Force (Army), Navy, Air Force, Air Defense Force, National Guard, Ministry of Interior Forces

Military age: 18 years of age

Military manpower, fit for military service:
Males age 15–49: 3,171,860 (1999 est.)

Military expenditures, dollars: $18.1 billion (1997 est.)

Military expenditures, percent of GDP: 12% (1997 est.)

Notes

1. Philip K. Hitti, *History of the Arabs*. 10th ed. New York: St. Martin's, 1970, p. 3.

2. Quoted in "Press Law 93," *Index on Censorship*, http://carryon.oneworld.org/index_oc/issue296/saudi.html, 1995.

3. "Press Law 93."

4. Eleanor Abdella Doumato, "Women and the Stability of Saudi Arabia," *Middle East Report*, July-August 1991, pp. 34–37.

CHRONOLOGY

1000 B.C.
Minean kingdom flourishing in southwestern Arabia.

100 B.C.
Nabatean kingdom established in the north of the Arabian Peninsula.

400s A.D.
Mecca becomes the leading city of Arabia.

570
Birth of Muhammad.

622
Muhammad and a band of followers flee Mecca and migrate to Medina.

630
Muhammad captures Mecca, marking the beginning of a period of expansion leading to the Islamic empire.

1400s
Saud dynasty founded in the region around modern Riyadh.

1517
Control of most of the Arabian Peninsula passes to the Ottomans.

ca 1750
Wahhabi movement begins in Najd in the center of Arabia.

1802
Mecca is conquered by the Wahhabis.

1812
Wahhabis are driven out of Mecca.

1818
Wahhabis and Sauds join to establish their capital at Riyadh.

1865
Sauds lose control of Riyadh and their realm is divided between different clans and the Ottomans.

1891
The Al Saud family exiled to Kuwait.

1902
Ibn Saud retakes Riyadh.

1906
Saud forces regain control over Najd.

1924
Ibn Saud takes Mecca without bloodshed.

1925
Ibn Saud takes Medina.

1926
Ibn Saud declares himself king of Hijaz.

1928–1930
The Ikhwan turn against Ibn Saud but are defeated.

1932
Ibn Saud unifies the conquered territories and names the new country Saudi Arabia.

1938
Oil is discovered in the eastern provinces.

1939
Oil production begins under the U.S.-controlled Aramco (Arabian American Oil Company); Ibn Saud initiates large-scale modernization.

1940–45
Saudi Arabia allows the United States to establish an air base at Dharan during World War II.

1951
An agreement with Aramco gives Saudi Arabia 50 percent of all earnings from oil.

1953
King Ibn Saud dies; he is succeeded by his son Saud.

1960
Saudi Arabia helps establish OPEC to help sustain international oil prices.

1962
King Saud transfers power to his brother Faisal; relations with Egypt are severed over Egypt's role in Yemen-based revolution.

1964
Prince Faisal officially replaces Saud as king.

1967
Saudi Arabia sends twenty thousand soldiers to fight in the Six Day Arab-Israeli War; Saudi Arabia normalizes relations with Egypt.

1973
Saudi Arabia plays a leading role in an oil boycott against Western countries that support Israel; world oil prices skyrocket.

1975
King Faisal is assassinated.

1979
Saudi Arabia severs diplomatic relations with Egypt after Egypt makes peace with Israel; a group of Sunni Muslims barricade themselves inside the Great Mosque in Mecca, forcing the Saudi army to retake the mosque with great loss of life.

1980
Saudi Arabia takes control of Aramco.

1982
King Khalid dies; he is succeeded by Fahd.

1987
Saudi Arabia resumes diplomatiic relations with Egypt; four hundred Iranian pilgrims are killed after clashes with Saudi security forces in Mecca.

1990
Iraq invades Kuwait; Saudi Arabia invites hundreds of thousands of foreign troops (mainly from the United States) to use Saudi Arabia as a base.

1991

Saudi Arabia is involved in air attacks on Iraq and in the land force that went on to liberate Kuwait.

1992

King Fahd proposes steps toward greater political expression in the kingdom.

1993

Saudi Arabia experiences severe budget deficits, mainly as a result of the Persian Gulf War.

1994

270 people die in Mecca during a stampede, raising international criticism of Saudi Arabia's ability to protect pilgrims.

1995

King Fahd has a stroke and the job of running the country falls mainly to Crown Prince Abdullah.

1996

King Fahd resumes control of state affairs; a bomb explodes at a U.S. military complex near Dharan killing nineteen and wounding over three hundred.

1999

For the first time, Saudi women attend the meeting of an official organization looking into expanding political expression in the kingdom.

Suggestions for Further Reading

BOOKS

James Blackwell, *Thunder in the Desert: The Strategy and Tactics of the Persian Gulf War.* New York: Bantam, 1991. This is a detailed report on the Persian Gulf War for anyone who wants to know more about the American and other troops that attacked Iraq and Iraqi fortifications in Kuwait from their bases in Saudi Arabia.

Leila Merrell Foster, *Enchantment of the World—Saudi Arabia.* Chicago: Childrens Press, 1993. A concise review of the major aspects of Saudi history, society, and economy.

T. E. Lawrence, *The Seven Pillars of Wisdom.* New York: Anchor/Doubleday, 1991. The monumental work that assured T. E. Lawrence's place in history as "Lawrence of Arabia." This book provides an epic military story and a lyrical exploration of the mind of a great man who helped shape the Middle East as it exists today.

David E. Long, *Saudi Arabia.* Gainsville: University Press of Florida, 1997. This book discusses Saudi Arabia from the Saudi point of view yet remains objective. It encompasses all facets of Saudi life including the land, people, religion, culture, history, politics, economics, and foreign policy.

Martin Mulloy, *Saudi Arabia.* New York: Chelsea House, 1998. This view of the country provides interesting and different perspectives in a well-illustrated book for middle school students.

William Spencer, *Islamic Fundamentalism in the Modern World.* Brookfield, CT: Millbrook, 1995. This clear, basic work aimed at middle school readers explains the beliefs

of Islam and the general nature of religious fundamentalism. Additional topics include the relationship between
Islam and the West.

WEBSITES

Miguel Cruz's "Inside the Magic Kingdom" (http://u.nu/
travel/country/sa). This site provides a personal look at
Saudi Arabia with lots of photographs accompanied by
informative stories.

Saudi Arabia Links (www.columbia.edu/cu/libraries/indiv/
area/MiddleEast/Saudi.html). This is a good list of links to
Saudi Arabian sites from the Middle East Studies Department at Columbia University in New York City.

Saudi Arabia Ministry of Information (www.saudiinfo/
main). This is another official Saudi government site, but
this one has more than 2,000 pages of information.

Saudi Arabian Embassy (www.saudiembassy.net). The official site of the Saudi government. More than the very general nature of the contents, the best reason to visit this site
is to get a feel for the way the Saudi government portrays
itself and the country.

Saudi Arabian Flag (www.theodora.com/flags/saud_arabia_
flags.html). This site is a good source for general facts and
pictures.

**United States Energy Information Administration/Saudi
Arabia** (www.eia.doe.gov/cabs/saudi.html). This site provides a detailed analysis of the oil industry in Saudi Arabia.

WORKS CONSULTED

Deborah Amos, *Lines in the Sand: Desert Storm and the Remaking of the Arab World.* New York: Simon and Schuster, 1992. This book provides an in-depth study of Saudi Arabia's and the rest of Arab world's political and social reactions to the Persian Gulf War.

Alexander Bligh, "The Saudi Religious Elite (Ulama) as Participant in the Political System of the Kingdom," *International Journal of Middle East Studies,* February 1985. A discussion of how the ulama influences political and social conditions in Saudi Arabia.

Eleanor Abdella Doumato, "Women and the Stability of Saudi Arabia," *Middle East Report,* July-August 1991. This book examines the role of women in Saudi Arabia.

John L. Esposito, *The Islamic Threat: Myth or Reality.* New York: Oxford University Press, 1996. This book, written by a leading scholar of Islam, analyzes the challenges presented by modern Muslim political movements and offers insight into the sources and diversity of the key Islamic movements and crises in the world today.

John S. Habib, *Ibn Sa'ud's Warriors of Islam: The Ikhwan of Najd and Their Role in the Creation of the Sa'udi Kingdom, 1910–1930.* Leiden, Netherlands: Brill, 1978. This is a scholarly work about the social, political, military, and economic aspects of how Ibn Saud used the Ikhwan to build his kingdom.

Philip K. Hitti, *History of the Arabs.* New York: St. Martin's Press, 1970. In this book by one of the leading authorities on Arab history, the pre-Islamic and Ottoman periods of Arabia are covered particularly well.

David Holden and Richard Johns, *The House of Saud: The Rise and Rule of the Most Powerful Dynasty in the Arab World.* New York: Holt, Rinehart, and Winston, 1981. The fascinating story of Ibn Saud's rise to power, along with the history of the Al-Sauds before and after him.

Paul V. Horsman, *The Environmental Legacy of the Gulf War*. London: Greenpeace Publications, 1992. This short book details the environmental catastrophe brought about by the Iraquis as they left Kuwait.

Albert Hourani, *A History of the Arab Peoples*. Boston: Harvard University Press, 1997. Many say this is the best history of the Arabs, and it covers Saudi Arabian history in depth. It is easy to read for such a comprehensive work.

David E. Long, *The United States and Saudi Arabia: Ambivalent Allies*. Boulder, CO: Westview Press, 1985. This concise book covers the historical, economic, and military relationship between these two countries.

Peter Mansfield, *A History of the Middle East*. New York: Viking, 1991. The author, a journalist and historian, explores the last two centuries in the Middle East and explains Saudi Arabia's evolving relationships with its neighbors.

P. M. Holt, Ann K. S. Lambton, and Bernard Lewis (eds.), *The Cambridge History of Islam, 1: The Central Islamic Lands*. London: Cambridge University Press, 1970. A scholarly, comprehensive work about Arabia before Islam.

William Spencer, *The Middle East*. Guilford, CT: Dushkin Publishing Group, 1995. A collection of thought-provoking articles and country studies that brings Saudi Arabia's position among other Middle Eastern countries into focus.

Robin Wright, *Sacred Rage: The Wrath of Militant Islam*. New York: Touchstone, 1986. Discusses the roots of Islamic terrorism and revolution.

Internet Sources

The Saudi Arabian Embassy. *Golf in Saudi Arabia?* 1998. www.saudiembassy.net/publications/magazine-summer98/golf.html.

———, *Doors to Hospitality*. 1998. www.saudiembassy.net/publications/magazine-summer98/doors.html.

INDEX

PICTURE CREDITS

ABOUT THE AUTHOR

William Goodwin is a graduate of the University of California at Los Angeles and also has undertaken graduate studies in biochemistry, education, and English at UCSB and UCSD. He has taught high school sciences, owned and operated a boating school, written scripts for educational videos, and built a 43-foot sailboat. He has also written advertisements for a biotechnology firm and currently is a health and fitness writer for a leading medical website. He was living in San Diego when he began this book and finished it in Birmingham, Alabama where he now lives with his wife, Donna, and stepdaughters Meg and Ashton. He is the father of two teenagers, Gideon and Marilyn. He has also traveled extensively and once drove his Land Cruiser across Saudi Arabia from the Persian Gulf to the Red Sea and back.